STANDING IN THE GAP

Standing
in the Gap

KEN GARDINER

KINGSWAY PUBLICATIONS
EASTBOURNE

ISBN 0 86065 336 6

Front cover photo: Tony Stone Photolibrary—London

Printed in Great Britain for
KINGSWAY PUBLICATIONS LTD
Lottbridge Drove, Eastbourne, E.Sussex BN23 6NT by
Cox & Wyman Ltd, Reading.
Typeset by Nuprint Services Ltd, Harpenden, Herts.

*To
the fellowship at 'Pip & Jim's'
with whom I first discovered and shared
this teaching*

Contents

	God Bless Chimney-Pots	9
1.	Understanding the Plan	12
2.	Understanding Our Heritage	27
3.	Hindrances to Prayer	40
4.	Spiritual Warfare	48
5.	In the Spirit and with the Spirit	65
6.	The Faith Principle	79
7.	Petition and Intercession	91
8.	The Where, the When and the How	102
9.	Worship, Praise and Thanksgiving	117
10.	Meditation and Contemplation	126
11.	What to Pray For	139
12.	Into Action	151
	Epilogue	156

I looked for a man among them who would build up the wall and stand before me in the gap on behalf of the land . . .

Ezekiel 22:30a

God Bless Chimney-Pots

It was bedtime and the little girl was saying her prayers. 'God bless Mummy and Daddy. God bless my little brother, and...and....' Searching for inspiration, she opened her eyes and looked through the window. Kneeling by her bed, only the roof of the house opposite was visible...'and God bless chimney-pots.'

That is the sort of story grandparents love to tell, and when it involves a little child we accept it happily. The trouble is that we bring the 'chimney-pots' attitude with us as we grow older. We 'say' prayers, instead of praying. We are not sure why we do it, except that we have an idea instilled in us that we 'ought' to, but it is usually an effort. Certainly we have little understanding of what our prayers accomplish or, if we are honest, what we really expect them to accomplish anyway.

Much of the blame for this must rest on the pastors and clergy of our churches. I dare to say that because I am one of them and must take my share of the blame. We exhort people to pray, but give very little teaching on how to do it. I suspect that this is because we feel we are not very good at it ourselves. I was taught very little about praying in my theological training. It may be that other colleges are better at this than mine, but I doubt it. Perhaps my tutors were not very good at it either, maybe because no one had taught *them*! So we all tell each other we ought to pray, but few of us feel competent to teach anyone else. Eventually, I determined to do something about it and decided I would plan a teaching course on prayer.

As soon as I began I realized that it was not as straight-forward as I had imagined. It isn't simply a matter of explaining a technique of how to do it. It seems to me that our prayers are more likely to be effective if they are in line with God's plan of working than if they are against it. So it is necessary to discover what God's plan is. How do we do that? And if it is *his* plan anyway, why does he need us to pray? Then again; will God really listen to our prayers? After all, isn't he the almighty, the all-knowing Creator? How can we, sinful human beings, get near enough for him to pay any attention?

I turned to Scripture to see what it taught about these things. That widened the area even more. The Bible speaks of praying *in* the Spirit and *with* the spirit; is there any difference? It stresses the important place of faith in receiving answers to our prayers: of hindrances and downright opposition from spiritual forces in the heavenly realm. There are illustrations of different forms of prayer —meditation, contemplation, praise and thanksgiving, petition and intercession.

As I prepared the course to teach others, I found my own ideas were changing radically. I became excited as I discovered, in Scripture, truths which had never been explained to me in my training. Then I became apprehensive. If my teachers had not shared these things, surely it must be because they had not known them. For, what I was discovering was so exciting that, had they known them, without doubt they would have wanted to teach them to their students also. But if my teachers did not know them, why should *I* discover them? Was I right?

10

As I began, a little tentatively, to share what I was learning, I was encouraged as one or two people told me they found an echo in their own experience, or an inner witness that these things were so. Certainly, my own prayer life changed fundamentally: I believe that I now know what I am about when I pray. So, I set down what I have discovered in the hope that it will ring bells with others also. I trust that it is truly scriptural: truly, in the sense that it is what I have drawn *from* Scripture, rather than what I have imposed upon it and then sought to justify from isolated texts. Indeed, what has encouraged me greatly has been to discover how consistent Scripture is in its teaching.

There is much I have yet to learn. I do not know how God responds when we ask him to bless our chimney-pots, nor how it affects them if he does. But I believe there are countless blessings awaiting us, just for the asking. When God's people cried to him in the past, he answered with power. We are his people today, in *our* time. I believe he is only waiting for us to call, for that power to be seen again.

1

Understanding the Plan

Late August and early September is the time, in Southern England, for the cereal harvest. The fields are golden or white with wheat and barley; the machines are busy and within days the landscape changes to stubble and bales of straw. But suppose you are in the area and suddenly come upon a farm where there is no activity, and day after day the crop becomes whiter and whiter, bleached by the sun. At last your curiosity gets the better of you and you go to the farm to enquire why the harvest is not being gathered. The door is opened by the farmer himself and, as soon as you have explained why you are there, to your astonishment he begins to thank you profusely. 'I've been longing for someone to call to ask me to begin to gather in my crops. I'll start at once.'

The situation is ridiculous. It is his harvest, not yours. Why should he wait until someone like you comes along to ask him to gather in the harvest for which he sowed the seed in the first place? Yet that is exactly the situation which Jesus sets before his disciples when he saw the crowds who were harassed and helpless, 'like sheep without a shepherd'.

The harvest is plentiful but the workers are few. Ask the Lord of the harvest, therefore, to send out workers into his harvest field (Mt 9:37–38).

I believe these words are the key to understanding God's plan for this world and the vital role given to man in order to bring it about. In talking of a Lord of the harvest, Jesus is obviously referring to his heavenly Father. Like the farmer in my illustration, there is a harvest which he longs to gather but apparently he delays until someone will ask him to send out workers. In saying this, Jesus is teaching:

(1) God knows the situation and has a plan.
(2) He reveals that plan to man.
(3) He waits for man to desire and then request that the plan be put into operation.

Lady Julian of Norwich understood this truth and expressed it beautifully over 600 years ago:

> I am the ground of thy beseeching:
> First it is my will that thou have it;
> And after, I make thee to will it;
> And after, I make thee to beseech it
>   and thou beseechest it.
> How should it then be that thou
>   shouldst not have thy beseeching?

Revelations of Divine Love, ed. Grace Warrack (Methuen).

I said that Christ's words about the Lord of the harvest are the key to understanding God's plan. If that is so, we can expect the whole of Scripture, from the very beginning, to contain that teaching: and so it does.

The principle explained

Most editions of the Bible have over a thousand pages—in some versions, well over this number. By page three everything has gone wrong: man has rebelled against his Maker; sin and death have entered the world; and everything is contaminated. Two pages are not very much from which to learn God's original plan for this earth and man's place in it. However, certain facts are there if we have eyes to see. Within just three verses (Gen 1:27–29) we are told at least two things about God's original purpose for mankind.

First, man has tremendous worth—just in his existence; for, unlike anything else, man was made in God's own image. Man is God-like.

Secondly, man is to exercise lordship over the whole of the rest of creation upon earth; indeed, over the very earth itself. He is not only to fill the earth, he is to subdue it.

We might expect that if anything needed to be subdued God would have done it himself. In fact, he delegates the task to man. God's orders are specific. Man is to rule over the fish of the sea and the birds of the air and over every living creature. Finally, God gives man 'every seed-bearing plant on the face of the whole earth and every tree that has fruit with seed in it'. So, man is to be lord over the whole animal, vegetable and mineral creation.

Man himself is under the lordship of God, subject and responsible to him. He is God's steward upon earth. His lordship over the rest of creation is a derived lordship. Seeing things from God's angle, God's original plan was to have his will performed on earth through man. We know that, while the created order of plant and animal life can reflect something of God's glory, they are unable to comprehend God. But man, who was made in God's image, was created capable of having fellowship with his

Maker and of knowing his will. While it is true that we must not read more out of Scripture than God has put into it, nevertheless I feel that the passage in Genesis 3, which speaks of God walking in the garden while Adam and Eve hid themselves from his presence, implies that it was not the first time God had come to share himself with them. The point of that incident is that this was the first time that the beautiful communion which existed between God and man had been broken. The picture is of the owner of some property coming to discuss with his farm-manager how things are going; what needs to be done and what the manager will need in order to carry out the orders of his master. However, the manager has flagrantly disobeyed his orders and is too frightened to appear.

In the case of the relationship between God and man, this disobedience has not only destroyed the relationship of trust between them, it has actually severed man from the only source of life itself. From God's viewpoint it means that he no longer has his steward or manager to receive his orders and carry them out on earth. However, God has not changed his pre-ordained plan of working. He will not act on earth to bring in his will without man's agreement and co-operation. In considering the purpose and the place of prayer it is essential to grasp this truth, so let me repeat it: *God will not act on earth to bring in his will without man's agreement and co-operation.*

Some may object, claiming that God is sovereign and will act as he himself decides, irrespective of man. But that is to misunderstand. It is true that God is sovereign, but he has deliberately limited himself to work through man. And who are we to deny him this self-imposed restriction, if that is his will? We have seen that man is infinitely precious to God. He, above all else, has been created in the image of God. Why, it is from mankind that the Father is to provide a bride for his Son. He respects and loves man too much to force his will upon him. The story about the fruit of the tree of the knowledge of good and evil shows God giving man a free choice. He may either love, and therefore obey God, or he may choose to reject him. Man uses that freedom to reject God, his love and his will. So man has changed. He is no longer innocent, he has rebelled against his Creator: in a word, he is a sinner. But God has not changed. If he gave man free choice to reject him, then it must be by man's free choice that he returns to him. It isn't as simple as that, of course. There is the whole problem of man's sin which has to be dealt with, and that cost the life of Jesus on the cross. But that is not the subject of our consideration at the moment. The point I am making is that God is limiting his sovereignty so that man may freely choose that his will be done.

God may, and thankfully does, act in what can be called a 'preliminary' way; begging man to return, pleading with him to call upon him to help. But he will not force himself on man. It may be argued that frequently in Scripture God is described as acting quite unasked in sending judgement and retribution upon mankind. But that is a consequence of man's rebellion. Man has already invited God's judgement by his very disobedience.

The principle operating

We have seen that it was God's intention from the very beginning to rule the earth through the willing co-operation of man. An illustration of this principle in operation comes in the story of Abraham interceding for the city of Sodom. The sin of that city is so appalling that God decides to destroy it. Almost as an aside we are given a picture of God saying to himself, 'I will share with Abraham what I am about to do, because he is my chosen vessel through whom I plan to bless every nation in the world.' As soon as Abraham learns what God plans for Sodom he begins to intercede. He does it by throwing back at God, as it were, what he knows of God's own character. 'There may be fifty righteous men in the city. It would not be right for the Judge of all the earth to destroy them with the wicked.' So God agrees not to destroy it if there are fifty righteous people to be found there. Abraham asks, 'What if there are forty-five there?' God agrees to spare it for forty-five. In the course of arguing, Abraham gets the figure down to ten.

Whenever I hear that story, I have a picture of God—who is Justice as well as Mercy—knowing he must act to judge the evil course of the people in that city: but saying to himself, 'If only someone would come and ask me to spare the righteous.' Rather like a parent who has threatened some punishment if his child disobeys, hesitating to carry it out, in the hope that the child will say sorry. As Abraham begins to plead, God rejoices to find on earth 'a man after his own heart'. Abraham does not claim any merit on the part of those for whom he intercedes, he simply refers to God's own character. God must be true to himself! Of course, with the greater revelation of God and his ways which we have, but Abraham did not, we know that the only ground on which God is able to have mercy is the offering of Christ on the cross for the sin of the world. However, that story of Abraham's intercession for Sodom clearly demonstrates the principle that God is waiting for man, at least one man, to stand before him and beseech him to act in mercy according to his own character and will.

God is always looking for a man to 'stand in the gap', as Abraham did, between the world's need of redemption, and God's willingness to give it, if only man desires it and will ask for it. God himself proclaims that fact through his prophet Ezekiel:

> I looked for a man among them who would build up the wall and stand before me in the gap on behalf of the land so that I would not have to destroy it, but I found none (Ezek 22:30).

Standing in the gap

So there is a gap between God's loving will and the world's need, which we may picture in this way;

We must now grasp a problem we have touched on in passing, but have not really faced. Even the Abrahams and Ezekiels of this world who dared to stand before God on its behalf were sinners. From the time of man's first disobedience all men have been contaminated, none is truly righteous; not one. If God was willing to overlook this temporarily, he could not do so permanently if he was to be true to his own righteousness; for all unrighteousness must be punished. It was 'divine forbearance' alone which allowed these men to stand in the gap on particular occasions, as Paul makes clear in his letter to the Romans (3:25).

The problem for God, therefore, was that he had limited himself to work his will in the world through man; but there was now no totally innocent man upon earth. Thus there was no perfect channel or vessel to bring God's will into effect. What is more, because man holds such a key or central position in God's plan, everything else in creation which, remember, was made subject to man's

18

rule or lordship, has been affected also.

The solution was for God himself to become man and, as man, perfectly to perform his own will.

That is exactly what Jesus did when he came to earth. Scripture describes it in this way:

The Word became flesh and lived for a while among us (Jn 1:14).

It is interesting that John does not say directly, as we might expect, '*God* became flesh' but refers to Jesus as 'The Word'. Now a word is what I need to convey something from my mind into your mind. It is something I use to express myself; what I am, what I believe, think, feel or desire. In that diagram four paragraphs back, we showed God's will like radio or television waves coming from a transmitter. God is constantly 'transmitting' his will; that is to say, he is eternally expressing himself. By saying, 'The Word became flesh,' John is trying to help us understand that Jesus was the very self-expression of God revealed as a human being. While Jesus lived here in the flesh, for the first time since man rebelled, God had a perfectly innocent man upon earth capable of receiving his instructions and willing to obey them.

When I was a little boy I was taught in Sunday School that Jesus performed his miracles and worked his mighty deeds because he was God. To be honest, I was taught that also when I was grown up—in fact, early in my ministry I myself taught it to others. I no longer believe that is true! Oh, I believe Jesus is God and even when he became flesh and lived among us he never ceased to be God; he couldn't, for that is what he is in his essential being. But when he came upon earth, he really did become a human being just as we are. The only difference is that he was sinless. (But what a difference that is!) So I no longer believe that he performed his miracles and works because he was God, but because he was perfect man. That is to say, he was so completely open to God that God was able to work his works through him. So Jesus perfectly fulfilled God's original intention that he should have his will done on earth through man.

Jesus constantly taught that he was not performing his deeds in his own power.

> The Son can do nothing by himself; he can do only what he sees his Father doing (Jn 5:19).
> The words I say to you are not just my own. Rather, it is the Father, living in me, who is doing his work (Jn 14:10).

Jesus is the one who 'stood in the gap' between God's perfect will and the needs of the world. The writer of the letter to the Hebrews expresses it most clearly of all:

> When Christ came into the world, he said.... 'a body you prepared for me.... then I said, "Here I am... I have come to do your will, O God"' (Heb 10:5–7).

Jesus, himself eternally God, comes upon earth and takes a human body. Then, as a man, opens himself utterly to his Father and says, 'You enter me! Live in me! Work your work through me; so that your will may be done perfectly on earth as it is in heaven.'

We can now redraw our diagram as follows:

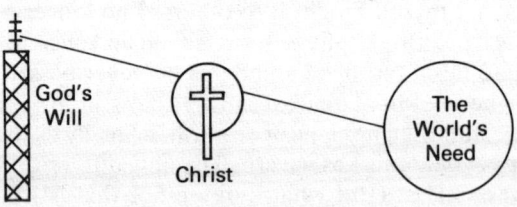

What is the situation now?

That is all very well for the period of about three years while Jesus carried out his ministry in the world: God's will was earthed—that is to say, his will was done on earth as it is in heaven, in and through the person of Jesus. However, after his crucifixion, Jesus rose from the dead and returned to his Father's side in heaven. So who can 'stand in the gap' now, in our age, to earth God's will?

The answer is simple but demanding:- that is our task, we who form the church! We are the body of Christ on earth. Before Christ came, God called individuals like Abraham, Moses and Isaiah, and gave them his Spirit so that he had someone to stand in the gap before him on behalf of his own people. But, as we have seen, this was only because of his divine forbearance. All of those individuals were sinners themselves and had no *right* to stand before him. As Scripture explains (Rom 4:3) God was willing to credit Abraham's faith to him as righteousness even though he had no actual righteousness of his own.

Now, however, we can see exactly how God has provided for a redeemed people on earth. We stand after the event; Christ has actually dealt with our sin on the cross. The staggering truth is that the church is to be on earth what Christ was during his earthly ministry. This truth is so staggering that many, even pastors and teachers, do not really believe it and so fail to preach and explain it. And if Christians are not taught it, they cannot act upon it, and thus a crucial part of God's plan for getting his will done on earth remains unfulfilled.

This truth is so important that I will explain it in a little more detail. There is a text in John's gospel which preachers rarely expound. It is something Jesus said to his disciples at the last meal he had with them on the night he was betrayed. In fact, Judas Iscariot had already left to fetch the soldiers to capture him.

> I tell you the truth, anyone who has faith in me will do what I have been doing. He will do even greater things than these, because I am going to the Father (Jn 14:12).

If you look at that carefully you will see that Jesus is saying that the things he did—the miracles and the teaching—would be done by anyone who believes in him. Not just the first disciples, or bishops or clergy or missionaries: *anyone who has faith in Jesus.* Presumably that includes you!

In fact, Jesus goes on to say they will actually do even greater things than he did. What is he talking about? We have already seen how Christ was able to do all his mighty works because he was perfect man utterly surrendered to God's will. It was 'the Father living in me, who is doing his work' (Jn 14:10).

Now if that is true; if it was God the Father working in the human body of Jesus doing those wonderful works, then, if only we could present our bodies to our heavenly Father as fully and freely as Jesus presented his body, it is conceivable that God could do the same works through us.

That is exactly what Paul exhorts Christians to do in his letter to the Romans. He spends eleven chapters explaining God's plan of redemption and then he urges them, in view of the mercy God has shown them:

> Offer your bodies as living sacrifices, holy and pleasing to God—which is your spiritual worship. Do not conform any longer to the pattern of this world, but be transformed by the renewing of your mind. Then you will be able to test and approve what God's will is—his good, pleasing and perfect will (Rom 12:1–2).

22

A book about prayer is not the place to pursue Christ's teaching on how we are actually to *do* the works he did—and greater works; although we shall return to the subject when we consider the important place of faith. However, in those two verses written to the Christians in Rome, Paul states that if we will offer our bodies as a living sacrifice to God, as Jesus offered his, and if we will allow the Holy Spirit to renew our thinking, then we shall know what God's will is. If we know it, then we can pray it into being on earth. What is more, if it *is* God's will, and we beg him to do it, to complete it, we can expect him to answer because it is what he has wanted to do in the first place.

To complete our understanding of what Christ taught about knowing God's will, let us recall what he said when he told the disciples that they would be able to do what he did (Jn 14:12). He went on to explain that this would be possible 'because I am going to the Father'. That statement was, in turn, amplified as follows:

> Unless I go away, the Counsellor will not come to you; but if I go, I will send him to you' (Jn 16:7).

Apparently, therefore, if Jesus goes away he will ask the Father to send them another Counsellor to be with them, and with all who believe in him. This Counsellor,

> The Holy Spirit, whom the Father will send in my name, will teach you all things (Jn 14:26).

So the last piece of the jig-saw falls into place. God now has a redeemed people capable of fellowship with him and to whom he can reveal his will. The original plan of exercising his purposes on earth through man can be brought into operation. The first Adam, who should have fulfilled that plan, was disobedient and failed. However,

> A second Adam to the fight
> and to the rescue came.
>
> (J. H. Newman)

Jesus came on earth as man and was perfectly obedient. At his baptism the Holy Spirit came upon him, and the Father was able to work his work through the Son by the power of that Spirit in him. Now Jesus has returned to heaven and, at his request, the Holy Spirit has been sent to come upon all who make Jesus their Saviour and Lord. We are to continue his work—not in our own authority and power any more than Jesus did it by his own authority and power (as he was careful to explain)—but in the power of his Holy Spirit, so that God may work his work in us. No wonder the church is called 'The body of Christ'—we are to be the vehicle, open to God, through which his will is to be done on earth as it was in Christ's human body. We can draw our diagram a third time like this:

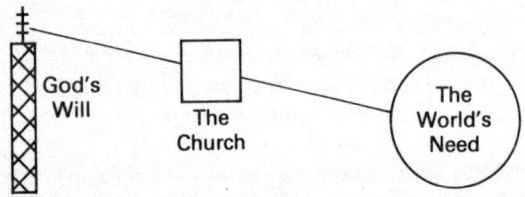

We are the ones who stand in the gap. First, we are to discern God's will—and that is part of prayer. Then we are to pray it into being on earth: begging the Lord of the harvest, who is the Lord of everything else as well, to fulfil that will; to make it happen on earth.

God is sovereign

When I first began to understand this truth—that God works his will on earth only through man's co-operation, I was shaken. I had been brought up to believe God is sovereign and it seemed to me that this teaching was a denial of his sovereignty. I have now come to understand that there is no conflict at all. God *is* sovereign, and this is the manner in which his sovereignty is worked out on earth. At first I feared that it detracted from his glory and majesty; now I see that, in fact, it enhances it. That an almighty God should, of his own will and good pleasure choose to limit himself in this way reveals a humility that is utterly foreign to human behaviour. God, the living God, has decided to involve—even to depend on—his creatures for his rule to be realized. Nevertheless it is all of a piece with a Lord who demonstrates his lordship by washing the feet of those who profess to follow and serve him. God does not force himself upon us. He waits for man to desire him. He teaches man to pray, 'Your will be done on earth.' He does not impose that will arbitrarily. Everyone in the kingdom of heaven is there only because he wants to be, having responded to the invitation of Christ, 'Follow me.'

Also, of course, this understanding of God's plan goes some way towards explaining why there is so much suffering in the world. So often people ask, 'Why doesn't God do something?' when there is a tragedy which a loving and almighty being could surely prevent. Perhaps he is longing to do something just as our fictitious farmer was longing to gather in his harvest, but he is waiting for someone to ask him to intervene. Maybe, even, to offer himself as Christ did, to be the agent through whom God can work his work on earth. Perhaps it is our lack of concern rather than God's which is holding up the relief of

25

so much pain, fear and horror in our world.

If, at the moment, you are not fully persuaded that Scripture does teach that God waits for man's co-operation before carrying out his will on earth, may I suggest you suspend judgement? Keep an open mind as you read on. I hope to build up the evidence chapter by chapter, revealing just how important man is in the plan of God and how much God loves us.

2

Understanding Our Heritage

Our attitude to ourselves

We all know what it means to enjoy good health, but there are some who enjoy bad health. I am not referring to those wonderful people who, in spite of suffering, manage to be cheerful. I mean those who literally enjoy being ill. They talk of nothing else. They do not want to be well—although they will claim that they do—because they would not know what to do with themselves if they were. They cannot face the responsibilities they would have to assume if they were well.

There is a similar problem with some Christians—those who appear to enjoy the fact that they are miserable sinners. There is a school of thought which proclaims that we are all miserable sinners and we shall go on being miserable sinners until we die. At first sight this teaching appears to show humility. It enhances the mercy and grace of God who is willing to accept us in spite of our sin. But this teaching undermines the plan and the work of God and it is unscriptural. The truth is that we *were* miserable sinners, but we are no longer so. The finished work of Christ on the cross is so complete, so effective, that if we have truly accepted him as Saviour and Lord a fundamental change has taken place; not only in our standing or relationship with him, but within our very being.

Before we were redeemed we were sinners by nature. It was natural for us to sin. Maybe we often did good things. We might keep a straight course for a while, but sooner or later we would go out of line. Everyone is born into this world with a bias to sin, much as a 'wood' in the game of bowls has a bias set into it. It runs straight for a while but inevitably that weight takes over and it swerves off course. In the game of bowls that, of course, is the intention. However, that tendency in man, every man, is described theologically as 'original sin'. We are now all sinners by nature, and that was not God's intention.

When we are born again of the Holy Spirit, we are given a new nature—that of God himself. Paul tells the Corinthians that if anyone is in Christ he is a new creation (2 Cor 5:17), the old order or nature has gone and a new one has come. John is even more specific. He says:

> No one who is born of God will continue to sin, because God's seed remains in him (1 Jn 3:9).

That word 'seed' is *sperma* in the Greek. Other translations say God's 'nature' is in us because we are born of his *sperma*. They also say boldly that we *cannot* sin. Some people have taken that to mean that it is literally impossible for a Christian to commit any sin and have preached 'instant holiness'. In fact, however, the tense of the verb shows that it is speaking of *continuing* to sin.

I'm sure you have experienced this truth in your own life. Before you were a Christian you could sin happily. Even when your conscience did prick you, you would deal with it by saying that it wasn't your fault or you only did whatever it was because someone else had first done something to you. Now that you are a Christian you will have learnt that you can no longer appease your conscience in this way. You need to confess your sin—certainly to yourself and to God—and if someone else has been harmed you will need to apologize and make reparation where possible. The reason for this is simple. Now that you are redeemed, though you may fall, you are no longer a sinner by nature: you have a new nature—God's. No wonder you cannot find peace with unconfessed sin within you; it is contrary to your new nature.

I appreciate that to an outsider this may seem to be splitting hairs. There may appear to be little difference between an unredeemed sinner who can do good things and a redeemed man with a new nature who can do bad things. In fact a fundamental change has taken place. We are no longer sinners by nature. We *can* sin but it is now foreign to our nature. Paul writes to the Roman Christians:

> Count yourselves dead to sin but alive to God in Christ Jesus (Rom 6:11).

That word 'count' is a technical term meaning to take account or to reckon. It is the word which lies behind our request for a statement of account at our bank. We look at it and see where we stand: are we solvent or in the red? Once we know the state of our balance we then decide what we can do. We may purchase a particular item or plan a holiday. We know our financial position. Paul is saying, therefore, 'Look carefully where you stand. Take full account of the fact that you are no longer a sinner. That nature died when you were baptized into Christ. You now have a new standing before God, *so have that standing in your own eyes also*. Take account of the facts!' We need to understand that when we repented of our sins, confessed them and made Christ our Saviour and Lord, not only were our past acts of sin forgiven, but the principle of bias of sin itself within us was dealt with. We are no longer sinners but children of God with his nature in us.

We need to renew our thinking and see ourselves as God sees us. To say that we are still miserable sinners does not enhance the glory of God. It denigrates the work of Christ by seeking to limit its effect to the forgiveness of past sins without recognizing the fundamental change which he has effected within us. When we were born again of God's seed, his nature was implanted in us, and that nature cannot continue to sin.

It is essential that we believe this, not only for our own well-being but for God's sake. We saw in the first chapter that God is looking for someone to stand in the gap to bring in his will on the earth. We are the ones to do that. We have been chosen for that very task. We are the essential link between all the blessing God desires to pour upon the earth and the desperate needs of the world in which we live. The world cannot call on God, but we can. We must not come cringing into the presence of God as though we think we have no right to be there. He desires us to come boldly and with authority as his sons. Unless we are convinced that we have that right we will not dare to do it and the world will be the poorer because we are not fulfilling the task for which we were created, redeemed and called.

God's attitude to us

> He [the Father] chose us in him [Jesus] before the creation of the world... (Eph 1:4).

When I was young I used to go shopping with my mother. I remember standing outside a butcher's watching

30

her select a joint of meat in the window. There was a plastic ticket stuck into it bearing the word 'choice'. As an adult I have grown cynical, but to me then it meant that of all the joints in the window the butcher had selected that as the very best. The fact that, as my mother bought that one, he simply stuck the label into the joint next to it was confusing but did nothing to destroy my illusion that we had obtained the very best joint of meat he had.

We Christians are not hunks of meat, but we do have a label on us—the seal of the Holy Spirit (Eph 1:13). God truly has selected us, chosen us, to be his. The verse at the head of this section tells us that God chose us even before he created the world. That is to say way, way back in eternity, before time began, God thought of us, planned for us to be. We are no afterthought, suddenly appearing on the scene, setting God a problem to find where he can fit us into his plan. The plan was there first and we are part of it.

Sometimes I meet a Christian who thinks he or she was 'a mistake'. A foolish parent has told them, 'I only married your father because you were on the way.' Perhaps you are in that very situation, and that has been said to you. Don't you believe it. Maybe your parents had not planned your creation, but God had. Whatever the morality of *their* action, God used it to get you into the world on schedule. You are no mistake. If you are a Christian, you were chosen by God in Christ before the creation of the world.

You may think that it was the other way round; you chose Christ. In a very real sense that is true. You have free will; if you didn't your offering of yourself would be of no value to God. As it is, God has set you free: free to respond to his love or to reject him. Your decision to respond to him, which if genuine is a total offering of yourself, is what delights God and makes that offering valuable. The disciples made that decision when they left their nets or tax-collecting to follow Christ. Nevertheless, Jesus said to them:

> You did not choose me, but I chose you (Jn 15:16).

And that is true of us also. God chose us before the foundation of the world to belong to Christ. Our offering of ourselves is a response to his choice of us in the first place. But there is a truth of particular importance in our consideration of prayer if we read the whole of that verse:

> You did not choose me, but I chose you to go and bear fruit—fruit that will last. Then the Father will give you whatever you ask in my name (Jn 15:16).

Jesus is saying that the purpose of his choosing men and women to be his is that they may bear fruit and obtain answers to their prayers. In other words chosen to 'stand in the gap', to serve.

It concerns me that many Christians concentrate almost exclusively on the wonder of the past and the future and seem to ignore the present. They rejoice, rightly, that their past sins are forgiven and that they have a sure and certain hope for the future in heaven. I do not wish to diminish in any way that assurance with the joy it brings. However, I am no longer living in the past nor have I yet attained the future. I am living *now* and I have been chosen by Christ to live for him now. It is a travesty of the gospel to see salvation as no more than lolling about in heaven when we die. Surely the parable of the talents (Mt 25:14–30) teaches us that we have to be about our Father's business here and now. (And, incidentally, the reward for faithful service in this life seems to be greater responsibility and service in heaven. So much for lolling about!)

The truth is that we have been hand-picked for service and the hand that picked us bears a nail mark. We are God's crack troops, his S.A.S. The ones who do not get into the news but who infiltrate the enemy's lines to prepare the way for others to follow. We are the ones to bring heaven down to earth: to get God's will done on earth as it is in heaven. For we live in enemy territory. The whole world is under the control of the evil one (1 Jn 5:19). Although we are in the world we are not a part of it (Jn 17:15–16). We are citizens of heaven (Phil 3:20) and are to live out our lives according to the laws of that kingdom. We are the kingdom troops. We are to live the kingdom, demonstrate the kingdom, draw others into the kingdom and pray the kingdom into being on earth.

God is not looking for clever people, strong people or important people. He is looking for obedient, willing people. Are you at your post, standing in the gap? Exercising dominion on the earth? Seeking to know God's will? Working, in prayer, to call it down? 'Faithing' it into being?

Our attitude to God

> You received the Spirit of sonship. And by him we cry, 'Abba, Father.' The Spirit himself testifies with our spirit that we are God's children (Rom 8:15–16).

While writing this book I was given a holiday in the Holy Land. On one of our trips I heard a cry behind me, 'Abba, Abba.' Turning round, I saw a little boy running after his father who had gone on ahead. To this day it is the word a child uses of his father: the equivalent of our term 'Daddy'. Paul is saying in that text above, 'When we are born again and come alive in the spirit, the Holy Spirit confirms to our spirit that God is our Daddy.' I must admit that in my own prayers I do not find it comes easily to use the word 'Daddy'; I prefer to say 'Father'. But I have learnt to think of God in a much more personal and intimate manner. After all, Jesus taught that we must become like little children if we are to enter the kingdom (Mt 18:3), so perhaps it would do us good if we were more prepared to lay aside our own cleverness and wisdom, which is so often of the world, and think of ourselves as little children, and God as our Daddy.

The story is told of the son of a great president. He was playing in the garden and fell and hurt his knee. He rushed into the house crying 'Daddy, Daddy', only to be stopped from rushing through a doorway by an official who said that the President was in conversation with a minister and must not be disturbed. 'He may be President to you,' said the lad, 'but he's my Daddy.'

God is the almighty, all-holy, all-knowing Creator of everything that is, but he wants us to come to him crying, 'Abba, Father.'

This understanding of our relationship with God is so important that I want to spend a little longer developing it further. The Good News Bible has a translation of a verse in the Book of Proverbs which I find simple but profound:

> Be careful how you think; your life is shaped by your thoughts (Prov 4:23 GNB).

What we believe about ourselves, about others and about God, will determine how we behave. If I think of myself as a miserable sinner who can never be anything else, I will never dare join God's S.A.S. to do battle for him in the world. If I see him *only* as an utterly holy Creator, far, far away in heaven, I will never even imagine I can come into his presence and ask for things, either for myself or the world. Certainly I will never dare to stand in the gap.

The trouble is that so many of us have been made to feel inadequate. Perhaps we had parents who were unable to show us very much love. Perhaps they were too busy, or inhibited in their own emotions, and while they *did* love us, they were unable to express it. This would have made us think that perhaps the fault lay with us and we are unlovable, creating in us a sense of insecurity. Perhaps at school we were not very clever and didn't do very well. It may be that our parents gave us the impression, consciously or unconsciously, that they very much wanted us to pass some exam and we didn't. This would have created in us a lack of significance. If we were useless at games as well, that view would have been strengthened. That verse from Proverbs tells us we must be careful how we think, because if we have a poor view of ourselves our whole outlook in life will be warped. We will believe that no one could love us—not really love us. Or that we cannot succeed at anything of real importance.

If you identify with this, Scripture explains very clearly what you need to do—renew your mind (Rom 12:2; Eph 4:23). It has been programmed wrongly with false information. You have picked up the idea that you are unlovable and useless. The truth is that God loves you so much that when he had the choice of either saving his own Son from the cross and losing you, or gaining you and allowing his Son to die, he chose you! The truth is that even before he made the world, he chose you to be his child for particular tasks which he had already prepared for you to do (Eph 2:10). He knew that in his strength, you were just the person to do them.

It is all very well explaining these truths as facts. You may be able to accept them with the top of your mind. The problem, so often, is that we have lived with the false programming so long that the wrong view of ourselves is deep-set in our subconscious and controls both our thinking and our actions. So how *can* we renew our minds?

Use your imagination

One way to renew our minds is to use our imagination. How strange we are. We allow our imagination to work overtime with regard to our lusts and our fears, but we do not use it in the way God intended. Imagination is a gift that God has given us, so we should not be afraid of developing it in a healthy manner. If ever you have been in hospital or had to wait for the result of some medical examination or X-ray, or if a loved one is unexpectedly delayed without being able to contact you, probably your imagination has gone into top gear and worked overtime. You are convinced you have some incurable disease, or you have your loved one rushed to hospital after some dreadful accident.

Years ago I had TB in both lungs and having been shown the X-ray I had pains in my chest. Someone told me that these couldn't be caused by the disease because we have no pain nerves in our lungs. I've never checked to see if that is true, but the pains ceased the moment I heard it! Imagination has a powerful influence upon our subconscious mind. Paul says:

> Whatever is true, whatever is noble, whatever is right, whatever is pure, whatever is lovely, whatever is admirable ... think about such things (Phil 4:8).

The word 'think' is the same one translated 'count' or 'reckon' that we considered in connection with believing we had died with Christ. Paul is talking about letting our minds dwell on these positive, healthy things.

Very often, when I am speaking on this matter of the use of our imagination, I will ask people to shut their eyes and picture a scene in their minds as I describe it to them. You obviously cannot shut your eyes as you read, but I will set out a picture in words and as you read, try to imagine yourself going through the experience I describe.

You are in some great and splendid building: a palace. There are long corridors with magnificent double doors on either side. You are walking along one of these with Jesus at your side. He has his arm round your shoulder and he is leading you. You come to a particular doorway and Jesus steps forward to open the door. Inside there is the most beautiful, wonderful light. You are aware that there is someone in the room. Jesus takes your hand and brings you into the room. Jesus speaks: 'Father, here is... (and he uses your name). You gave him (her) to me and now I have brought him (her) to you.' The great and glorious Being looks at you and, as it were, smiles: 'So at last you have come to me. You have known my Son for a long time, and I know you love him, as I do. And I love you also. I have always loved you. It was I who loved you into being. I formed you in the womb and gave you your life. Come to me.' You leave the side of Jesus and walk towards the throne. This wonderful Being reaches down, picks you up in his arms and sits you on his knee. 'Now, tell me about yourself. Tell me all about your hurts and fears; the times you have wanted to give up, and run away and hide.' Perhaps you want to ask him about some loved one who is not yet a Christian, or bring the needs of the sick or underprivileged. But he stops you short—'I know, I know; but first, what about *you*? How are *you*? Let's enjoy each other's company for a while.' Imagine yourself telling him all the things you have kept to yourself for so long. Your sense of failure, rejection, or loss; and let him wipe away the tears from your eyes.

Some may be able to use their imagination in this way very easily. Others may want to skim over that rapidly and say it is not for them; they are not the type that sort of thing appeals to. If you come into the latter group, may I gently ask you to stop a moment and think why that is? It may be that in the past, possibly from the time you were a child, you were discouraged from showing your emotions. We in Britain are particularly bad about that. There is the 'stiff upper-lip' brigade, who never show what they feel and are very embarrassed if anyone else does. You may want to say that it is ridiculous that at your age you should try to imagine yourself sitting on anyone's knee. But if you rarely did this as a child, you need to experience it. Paradoxically, if you *did* do it as a child, you will probably have no difficulty about doing it now in your imagination. It is those who find it difficult who most need to do it.

Do practise this sanctified use of your imagination, especially as you read Scripture. Bring the stories to life. That scene I described above is based almost entirely on various texts of Scripture. Scripture itself is full of vivid appeals to the imagination. In Hosea (chapter 11) God pictures himself dealing with his people like a father teaching his little boy to walk. Jesus describes the people of Jerusalem as chicks whom he longs to protect in the way that a mother hen gathers her brood under her wings (Mt 23:37). As we picture ourselves truly acting as trusting children, happily running in and out of our heavenly Father's presence, so our subconscious mind will be renewed as the Holy Spirit applies this truth deep in our being.

I have discovered that many Christians have comparatively little difficulty in relating to Jesus, but have very little sense of relationship with God the Father: their Father. Certainly they cannot truly say 'Abba, Father' to him. Usually this is because they had a poor or non-existent relationship with their earthly father. Perhaps he had a job which took him away from home for long periods, or he died early, or he left the family for someone else. Perhaps he was a drunkard, beat their mother or even sexually molested them when they were young. I have discovered these things are far more common than I had ever realized. No wonder such people find it difficult to imagine a heavenly Father. The very word 'Father' conjures up all sorts of unhappy memories and forms a mental barrier. To such people, Jesus is all they want to know of God. Yet he came to bring us to the Father.

You may feel I have taken too long and gone too far in stressing the need to get our relationship with God sorted out in our understanding. You want to get on with the practicalities of prayer. But remember the whole thrust of what Scripture teaches. God is looking for people who will stand in the gap which exists between himself and the world in which we live. In the world we have to take on the role of hand-picked troops. But we need also to enter the courts of heaven. We need to come with confidence, boldly to the throne of God that we may find grace to help in the time of need—the world's as well as our own (Heb 4:16). We shall never be able to do that effectively unless we are convinced in our subconscious that we have a right to be there.

How it must hurt the Father if we go on seeing ourselves as miserable sinners and God as a million miles away— loving, but distant. I believe God says to such people, 'You have not really understood what happened on the cross.' How sad if Jesus had to go through all that and we do not make use of all that he has won for us. God is still looking for people who will take him at his word and in spite of their own weakness and failure will dare to believe and say, 'He may be Almighty God—but he is my Father.'

3

Hindrances to Prayer

It is good to be positive and so I do not want to devote
much space to considering the attitudes and circumstances which cause problems as we seek to pray. Nevertheless, there *are* hindrances and we need to be aware of
them.

I am tempted to say that our greatest hindrance is our
bed. We do not want to get out of it in the morning and
cannot wait to get into it at night. Of course, the problem
does not lie with the bed but within the will. Remember
we do not 'find' time to pray, we have to make it. Nor do
we always 'feel' like praying—very often we have to do it
solely because we know it is essential:—God needs
someone to 'stand in the gap'.

I love my work as a vicar; I think I have the most
wonderful job in the world. Nevertheless, there are tasks
which I find boring or unpleasant. I know that they are
part of my work, so I just get on and do them. Prayer is
work. There will be times when you get down to your
prayer for no other reason than that you know it must be
done. Perhaps that does not sound very spiritual, but I am
certain God would rather you were at your post in prayer
simply because you believe it is important, than that you
were not there at all.

Doubt

This undermines our determination to pray. Perhaps we doubt that prayer does any good—especially if we see no immediate answers. Or maybe we doubt that God will listen to *us*. We believe he does answer prayer—for other people, but not us. But remember who you are, a child of God. You have the right to come into his presence saying, 'Abba, Father.'

Then, it can be that we doubt God's plans for us. We are worried that we might not like them. 'If I really pray "God's will be done", he will have me out in a mud hut in the middle of some jungle.' How strange we are. Why will we not believe that God desires the very best for us? If he really *does* want us in that jungle hut, then that is what he created us for and we will never be truly happy or fulfilled anywhere else. If we are married and have a family, God knows that; he knows our responsibilities better than we do. God tells his people in the Old Testament that he knows exactly the plans he has for them. They are for their welfare not their harm. He has planned a future full of hope (Jer 29:11). God has not changed. We are his people today and his plans for us are the very best. He desires our highest good. Never doubt that.

Fear

Fear is stronger than doubt. We may pray about a particular matter and doubt that God will answer; but also we may pray and fear that the exact opposite will happen. Doubt niggles at faith: fear overwhelms it. Faith is the channel through which God's blessing flows. Fear blocks that channel. In fact, fear can actually bring on the very thing we fear. Certainly, in the realm of our physical health, fear can cause all sorts of chemical reactions which, if prolonged, create conditions which promote disease. Job hit the nail on the head when he said:

> What I feared has come upon me;
> What I dreaded has happened to me (Job 3:25).

I am told that the words 'Fear not' appear 366 times in the Bible; one for each day of the year, including leap year! God knows how easily we can fall into fear and encourages us to trust him. In the sermon on the mount Jesus tells us not to have any anxiety about our daily needs: food, drink and clothing (Mt 6:28–34). If you read that passage carefully you will see that what he is telling us to do is to jump over the thing we fear into the arms of God. If we will concentrate on fulfilling the role he has given us, *he* will see we have what we need. Let us throw ourselves utterly upon the Lord in perfect trust.

Sin

Of course I could have put doubt and fear under this heading because anything contrary to God's will is sin. Certainly it is not his will that we should either doubt or fear. However, I am thinking now of specific attitudes and deeds which we choose to allow ourselves.

The psalmist gets to the heart of the matter:

> When I did not confess my sins,
> I was worn out from crying all day long....
> I decided to confess them to you,
> and you forgave all my sins (Ps 32:3,5 GNB).

We must recognize the difference between guilt and conviction. Guilt paralyses but conviction, if we act upon it, provides the way to a cure. Of course, if we have wronged someone it is not sufficient to confess it to the Lord only. We must do all we can to restore the relationship with that person. If they have died, or for some other genuine reason we cannot make our peace with them or their family, then of course we can trust in the full forgiveness of God alone.

Unconfessed sin makes prayer impossible. A moment's thought will reveal why. Scripture tells us that God's eyes are too pure to look on any sin (Hab 1:13). Yet we have seen that we need to be the link between God's will and the world's need. We *must* get into that throne room boldly and confidently. If we have unconfessed sin in our lives, we will never get off the earth, let alone through the door.

> Who may ascend the hill of the Lord?
> Who may stand in his holy place?
> He who has clean hands and a pure heart (Ps 24:3–4).

Forgiving

Most of us, most of the time, may avoid the very obvious outward sins such as murder, stealing, adultery and the like. Even so we may kill someone's reputation with our words; present other people's work or ideas as our own; or feed on lustful books or programmes on television.

However, there are many less obvious sins which set up barriers to our prayers. Jesus taught that one of the biggest barriers is our unwillingness to forgive. It is very interesting that in one of the passages which preserves some of his most specific teaching about prayer (Mk 11:20–24), which we shall examine in more detail when we come to consider the place of faith, he immediately goes on to stress the importance of our willingness to forgive.

And when you stand praying, if you hold anything against anyone, forgive him (Mk 11:25).

In the mind of Jesus, there is obviously a link between effective prayer and our willingness to forgive others. Notice he refers to *any*thing against *any*one and he does not put the stress on what they have done but on our holding something against them. It isn't so easy for us to wriggle out of that. This matter of forgiving others is absolutely crucial. Resentment blocks our prayers. If we are truly penitent, God forgives us anything and everything. How can we come to his throne if our attitude is different from his own? There is that within each of us which would want to say, 'But they wronged me.' If they hadn't, there wouldn't be any need for you to forgive, would there? That is the point of forgiveness. Have you discovered yet that the deepest reason why you must forgive is for your sake and not theirs? The real problem is what your resentment does to you rather than to them. It is blocking your walk with God, not theirs. Indeed, God forgives us 'for his name's sake', not ever ours, because he is love. We need to repent and receive that forgiveness if we are to benefit from it, but God is already clear of resentment—he never had any. Of course, it is costly to forgive; the other person has hurt us. But think what it cost God to forgive us—six hours of agony on the cross, and the physical agony was not the half of it.

Relationships

Another area of hindrance to prayer which is mentioned in Scripture is a breakdown of family relationship, especially between husband and wife.

> Husbands...be considerate as you live with your wives, and treat them with respect as the weaker partner and as heirs with you of the gracious gift of life, *so that nothing will hinder your prayers* (1 Pet 3:7).

I know the truth of this in my own experience. There has been more than one occasion in my life when I've had a disagreement with my wife and have tried to pray. It is no use. I cannot concentrate. I might just as well swallow my pride and get things sorted out with her immediately, because I won't get through to God until I have.

Incidentally, it is important that husband and wife do pray together. Not all the time, of course, but certainly for a brief period each day. How sad it is if they share other areas of their lives but not this spiritual experience of prayer. There is no doubt in my mind that Scripture puts the responsibility for ensuring that this happens upon the husband. In far too many Christian homes it is the wife who has to take the spiritual lead. The husband needs much encouragement and support from his wife, but the responsibility for the spiritual life of the family falls to the man. I suppose the point of that quotation above from 1 Peter is that you can hardly expect to get the kingdom going in the world if you have not first got it going in your own home.

Materialism

It seems so obvious that we will not get very far in praying for God to transform the world if we ourselves are tied to the world and its ways. Nevertheless, it is all too easy to love the world more than the kingdom.

In the Old Testament, the law was that God's people were to tithe, give a tenth part of whatever they gained, to God. This was not a free-will option, it was part of the law. The 'free-will' offerings did not start until the tithe had been paid. We are under grace not law. However, living under the new covenant and knowing, as people under the old did not, what it cost God to redeem me, the price he paid; I cannot under grace freely give less than they were compelled to give under the law. For over twenty-five years since we committed our lives to Christ, my wife and I have made our tithe, and more than the tithe, the first charge on our income. It hasn't always been easy, but we have never been in absolute want. Sometimes God has had to give *us* money, through someone else, to get us over a difficult period, but always we have put him first and he has never failed us. Unless we are willing to do this we are not giving God the opportunity to provide for us and we never experience the wonder of his faithfulness.

The prophet Malachi states very clearly that our unwillingness to give of our finances is a major cause of God withholding his blessing. It isn't that we are 'buying' God's blessing; rather, we are showing ourselves, as well as God, that we really do believe he is on the throne; we're not just saying it. In a very real sense it is a matter of putting our money where our mouth is.

Health

If we are off-colour, we find it difficult to do anything. Everything is an effort—including prayer. If you have ever been a patient in hospital you will know it is incredibly difficult to pray. However, this may be due to the countless distractions there are as much as to the illness we experience, and for many people confinement to bed or to the home has proved a wonderful opportunity for prayer. When we are deprived of the opportunity for action, the one thing above all that we can do is to pray.

Fortunately, however, the majority of us are not ill

most of the time, and surely we have a duty to do all that we can to keep ourselves in good health. Those who are experts in prayer sometimes liken it to exercise, saying that we need to keep our spiritual faculties as active and practised as our physical ones. Many of us Christians are not as physically fit as we should be. Man is a whole—body, soul and spirit—and all three interrelate. Our mental anxiety can produce a physical malfunction or stomach ulcer. If we are overweight—and gluttony is a sin which needs to be corrected as well as confessed—or if our bodies are not functioning as they should, this may make us lethargic and less alert in our prayers.

My wife marked our last wedding anniversary by giving me a skipping-rope!

4

Spiritual Warfare

'Is that you, Daddy? Are you free this afternoon? There's a girl here who has been involved with witchcraft: can I bring her home?'

My daughter was telephoning one lunchtime just before Christmas. It was the last day of the college term and some of the students had gathered in a nearby pub for a celebration. Under the loosening influence of two or three drinks, one of the girls had opened up to a friend that she was deeply involved in the occult and would like to be free of it. She was persuaded to come to see me, but at the door she refused to come in. She was frightened and obviously regretted having shared so much—little as that was—with anyone. It was cold and we managed to coax her indoors for a cup of coffee. As soon as I could do so I brought the conversation round to the reason for her coming: her involvement with the occult. She immediately clammed up and said she would like to leave. I wasn't sure what to do because obviously I had no right to keep her in our home against her will. So I said, 'Well, just before you go I would like to pray for you,' and, without waiting for an answer, launched into a prayer.

The effect was startling. I cannot recall anything of what I said. In fact, I had hardly said anything at all when I was aware of a profound change in the girl's breathing which had become very heavy and laboured. I opened my eyes and discovered that hers were closed and both her hands had adopted a strange configuration. The thumbs and two centre fingers were pressed inwards against the palms, but the first and little fingers were extended outwards. I learned later that this apparently depicts 'the horned god' of witchcraft. As she seemed to have lost control of herself I drew back her eyelids to reveal her pupils at the very top of her eyes: she was in a trance.

I had had a little experience of dealing with people involved in the occult, in fact I had attended a residential conference arranged by the Bishop of Exeter's Commission on Exorcism, but I had never met anything like this before. It transpired that this girl was very deeply involved indeed. As a child she had been taken to a spiritualist healer and medium. Later, a schoolteacher introduced her to black magic and witchcraft. From there she went on to satanism. She had been through a ceremony where, having renounced her Christian baptism, she was baptized into satanism and given a satanic name—a deliberate travesty of bestowing a Christian name—and had eventually gone through a satanic wedding where she had 'married' Satan. On various occasions she had invited certain spirits to enter her, to possess her; and she became a priestess with strange, occult powers.

In my home, while she was in a trance, as I prayed and commanded any evil power to leave, she spoke with a man's voice. In fact, over the next few hours that she was with us she spoke in a number of different voices. One by one the spirits left her, screaming as they did so. She was in need of far greater ongoing care than we could provide, and eventually she was taken for a period into a Christian community home which specialized in helping those seeking to break free of drug addiction.

I do not set out that story for sensation or to frighten. To be honest, the whole subject of spiritual warfare is one I would prefer to avoid, for I do not enjoy it. However, it is a vital area and no study of prayer would be complete without information about what it is. I have included that story to explain why I am convinced of the reality of Satan; I know from personal experience that Scripture is true when it says:

> Our struggle is not against flesh and blood, but against the rulers, against the authorities, against the powers of this dark world and against the spiritual forces of evil in the heavenly realms (Eph 6:12).

There are many today who would refute that. They would say that Paul, who wrote it, and Jesus himself, who taught the reality of Satan, were men of their times and in those times everyone did believe in a personal devil, in demons and in fallen angels: but, we in our enlightened age (so such people argue) know better than that. Don't you believe it!

Satan must be delighted at such teaching. Already he has the advantage of being invisible to us, but for Christians not to believe he exists is to give him an added bonus. Evil is much more than the absence of good. There are active, powerful and personal forces in the spiritual realm working to thwart God and his will for this world.

Scripture is consistent in what it teaches about Satan, but the information is scattered through the books of the Bible written by different people. Let me set out what the teaching is and where it can be found and then, of course, you must decide whether or not you accept it.

Heavenly powers—what Scripture teaches

Man is not the only created being. In fact, if we think about it, it may be presumption on our part to assume that we are. Scripture speaks of angels, cherubim and seraphim, principalities and powers, world rulers and spiritual hosts of wickedness. What is more, there is, as we shall see, a very clear authority structure in the heavenly realm, with some angels having specific areas of responsibility over other powers. Very often, in everyday conversation, you will hear people who make no particular claim to be Christian or even religious, refer to their 'guardian angel'. There is scriptural backing for this. On one occasion Jesus was using a little child to illustrate a point he was making and he went on to say:

> See that you do not look down on one of these little ones. For I tell you that their angels in heaven always see the face of my Father in heaven (Mt 18:10).

If Jesus simply meant that children have a special place in the care and concern of the Father, it is unnecessarily cumbersome to introduce the description of there being special angels in the Father's presence who have some particular relationship with those children (*their* angels). It seems that Christ was deliberately teaching that there are angels who watch over us. Whether they are indeed 'guardians' we are not told. However, they must be set there for a purpose and presumably that purpose, having the Lord's acceptance, must be good.

Then it seems that individual churches have their angels also. In the opening chapters of the book of Revelation John is instructed to write to seven churches active at that time. He is to list what pleases and displeases the risen, ascended Christ regarding their conduct. In each case John is instructed to write 'to the angel of the church in...". Of course, that raises a difficulty. How do you write to an angel? One way to overcome the problem is to translate the word as 'messenger' instead of 'angel'. This is perfectly legitimate because that is what the word means, and it is sometimes translated in this way elsewhere in Scripture where it applies to ordinary human beings (Lk 7:24 and 9:52). However, the term occurs sixty-seven times in the book of Revelation and, apart from the uncertainty in the first three chapters, there is no doubt that in every other case it refers to heavenly beings.

Some commentators assume it must refer to the bishops or pastors of the churches involved; but that is a rather strange way to describe them. (Are *all* bishops angels?) The word is not used in that manner elsewhere. I prefer to take it at its face value and believe it is referring to a heavenly being who has been given some spiritual responsibility or care over a particular church.

The book of Revelation falls within a group of writings which the scholars have named 'apocalyptic'. The name isn't important for our purposes, but it refers to scriptures which attempt to present truths about heaven in a form which can be grasped by our human minds. The letters which John was instructed to write were given to him in an astonishing, almost blinding vision of the Lord Jesus Christ in his glory. It is as though John was mid-way between heaven and earth, and it does not surprise or cause me concern that descriptions and metaphors become rather mixed in his desire to convey what he experienced. If, as I have come to believe, there are heavenly beings, angels, watching over each church, and if those churches need guidance, rebuke or exhortation, then I am not perturbed if John says he has been told to write to the angels of the churches involved, for it conveys a great and encouraging picture of what is going on 'behind the scenes'.

Angels over nations

Whatever you believe about those references to 'angels of the churches' in the book of Revelation—and there is legitimate reason for Christians to hold different views—we are on surer ground when we look at the book of Daniel. Once again, it is in the apocalyptic tradition, but this time from the Old Testament.

I must explain at once that scholars disagree about when it was written. It gives the impression that it was written at the time when the Jews, God's chosen people, were in exile in Babylon round about 600–500 BC. However, for various reasons, many scholars believe it was actually written about 165 BC. This is not the place to argue the case one way or the other. What is of importance to us is not so much when it was written, but, is what was written true? In particular chapter 10?

Once again, as we expect in apocalyptic writing, there is a description of what is going on 'behind the scenes' in the heavenly realm. Daniel is a man who walks closely with his God and is given many revelations of God's will—he was one who 'stood in the gap'. Apparently he had been given a vision or message which he did not understand and so he fasted and meditated in order to grasp the meaning. After three weeks (and he gives the precise date) he has a vision of a heavenly being who tells him that he has come in response to his prayer for understanding. In fact, he says, he would have been with Daniel much earlier but 'the prince of the Persian kingdom resisted me twenty-one days' (Dan 10:13). He wouldn't have got through even then had not Michael (whom he calls 'one of the chief princes') come to his aid.

As he gives his explanation, we are provided with an extraordinary picture of conflict in the heavenly realm with good angels, who are God's messengers and warriors, striving against rebellious angels, who are doing all they can to disrupt any link between heaven and earth. What is particularly interesting is that apparently each nation has its guardian angel—or prince, as the term is. The Jewish nation has a chief prince, Michael: 'Michael, the great prince who protects your people' (Dan 12:1).

So far, we have seen that Scripture teaches:

(i) There are 'guardian angels' for individuals
(ii) There may be 'guardian angels' for churches
(iii) There are 'guardian angels' (princes and chief princes) for nations.

With regard to (iii) there is no question that Scripture teaches this, but some would not accept this teaching as true.

A prince over the world

Now we go one stage further. If individuals have heavenly angels and nations have heavenly princes, we might expect there would be a more senior prince still, with responsibility for the whole world. This is exactly what we find. Jesus refers to Satan as 'the prince of this world' (Jn 14:30). Further light is thrown on this if we recall the temptations Jesus suffered in the wilderness. In the course of this experience the devil takes him to a high place and, in an instant, displays all the kingdoms of the world, saying:

> I will give you all their authority and splendour, for it has been given to me, and I can give it to anyone I want to. So if you worship me, it will all be yours (Lk 4:6–7).

I used to assume that Satan was here telling lies. The kingdoms of the world did not belong to him, they belonged to God. But then I realized that if that were so, there would have been no serious temptation to Christ at all. He had only to say, 'They are not yours to give,' and the offer was exposed as a hollow prize. In fact, of course, what made the temptation so glitteringly attractive was that the kingdoms of the world had indeed been given to Satan to rule in the spiritual realm. Jesus had come to do battle to gain them; a battle which was to culminate in the horror of his death on the cross. But here was Satan offering to give him the kingdoms if only he would, in turn, accept Satan as King. To avoid the cross, yet gain the world! That was why it was so great a temptation. Both Satan and Jesus knew that Satan had indeed been made 'prince of the world'.

Satan's origin

There can be no doubt from Scripture that if Satan exists at all—and I have already declared my own conviction that he does—he was created by God. Everything was created by God and without him nothing was made that was made. What is more, originally he must have been created perfect. God creates nothing evil. Presumably Satan, like mankind, had free will: his obedience to God was to be a free-will obedience. Apparently he was given spiritual authority or responsibility for the world—possibly akin to the way in which man was given dominion over the animal, vegetable and mineral creation. The plan was for God to effect part of his purpose and rule through the loving obedience of 'the prince of this world', just as another part of that purpose and rule was to be effected through the loving obedience of man.

We do not know why Satan rebelled against God—there are hints that it may have been pride in his own beauty and power. However, it isn't important that we know the details of that rebellion, it is enough that we know it happened. It was then that he became 'Satan', because the word is not really a name at all. It is a description and means 'the adversary'. He is implacably set against God.

Here it may be helpful to explain the careful authority structure that there is in God's order and economy. We see it in God's dealing with mankind. When he appoints a leader he will not countenance rebellion against that leader. On a number of occasions, for instance, some of the people challenged Moses—even his own brother and sister did so (see Numbers 12)—and God dealt with them in no uncertain terms. It is the same in the spiritual realm. There is a very interesting illustration of this in the letter written by Jude which is included in the New Testament. The reason Jude writes his letter is because some false teachers have got in among the Christians and he warns them to be on their guard against these godless men. One of the charges he levels against them is that they reject authority and slander celestial beings. As an example of how they should respect God's authority structure, Jude states:

> Even the archangel Michael, when he was disputing with the devil about the body of Moses, did not dare to bring a slanderous accusation against him, but said, 'The Lord rebuke you' (Jude:9).

Do you see what Jude is saying (and, incidentally, how utterly consistent Scripture is in its teaching about heavenly powers and rulers)? Although Michael is an archangel ('chief prince' is what Daniel called him), and therefore senior to other angels or princes, even he would not personally accuse or rebuke the devil. This is because, although he is the guardian prince of a complete nation— God's own chosen people, the Jews—Satan is the Prince of the whole world and therefore his senior.

When Satan rebelled against God, a host of lesser princes and angels followed him. We have seen how, in the book of Daniel, one of these, the 'prince of the Persian Kingdom', tried to prevent God's messenger getting through to Daniel, and how a chief prince (Michael) had to come to deal with him.

I realize, of course, that to anyone who has never examined the Bible's teaching about the 'spiritual forces of evil in the heavenly realms' against which we are fighting, this will all come as a shock. It is almost too astonishing to believe: but Jesus believed it and so did those who have given us the New Testament.

Why doesn't God act?

If Satan is so powerful and is causing so much disruption, why doesn't God act against him? The answer is that he *has* acted, but in order to comprehend just what he has done we need to understand the present situation more clearly.

We have seen that, whatever the reason, Satan is now in utter rebellion against God. Because God himself is his creator and all-powerful, Satan cannot get at God directly. All he can do is to seek to hurt and destroy what God holds dear.

I remember being involved in a sad situation some years ago. A young man, who was particularly bitter and vindictive, held a grudge against his mother. He did not dare lay a finger on her, but she had a dog which she loved dearly. If she was in the room he would kick it, because he knew that in hurting the dog he was hurting her.

God loves man—infinitely. So, knowing that God has given man free will, Satan sets about tempting man to rebel against God's love; and man succumbs. Of course, God could destroy Satan; but in doing that he would not be true to himself unless he also destroys man. He has already stated that disobedience must involve judgement and death (Gen 2:17). So Satan is in a strong position; he is holding man hostage. If there is to be any hope for man at all, God has to find a way to get man away from Satan. The only weapon God has is love. In fact, as Scripture says:

> God so loved the world that he gave his one and only Son, that whoever believes in him shall not perish but have eternal life (Jn 3:16).

and Jesus, himself, explained that he had come

> to give his life as a ransom for many (Mk 10:45).

In some wonderful way, Christ dying on the cross as man satisfied the demands of justice and of judgement. If man's disobedience brought death, one man's obedience brought life—or, at least, the opportunity of life.

So the situation is this. Everyone is born a sinner: we all disobey God sooner or later. To put it in human terms, Satan can say to God about each of us, 'That's another who has failed you, so he belongs to me, not to you. He must die, according to your own decree.'

However, since Christ's victory on the cross, his resurrection and ascension, there is a way out. Of course, man has to choose to take it, but the opportunity is there. We take it, we make the choice, when we make Jesus Christ our Lord and accept him as our Saviour. Again, to put it in human terms, Jesus can say to Satan, 'You did all in your power to tempt me, as man, to reject God and his will. You failed. I went to the cross and there I died for every man. Your final power is the power of death: I have defeated that. You have been disarmed. Now every man who chooses to do so may come to me. You must let them go for they have responded to my love and they are mine.'

Satan has to let them go because he knows full well that Jesus did indeed win the victory on the cross. As Paul explains it in his letter to the Christians at Colosse:-

> God made you alive with Christ...having disarmed the powers and authorities, he made a public spectacle of them, triumphing over them by the cross (Col 2:13–15).

Notice that 'the powers and authorities' have been disarmed. In defeating Satan, all those who serve him are disarmed as well.

The time will come when Satan is to be dealt with once and for all (Rev 20:10). What is more, Satan knows it, and so do at least some of his followers (Mt 8:29). Scripture is very clear that Satan knows he has little time left. He is determined to cause as much harm as he can to God and his kingdom, in the time that remains to him:

> But woe to the earth and the sea, because the devil has gone down to you! He is filled with fury, because he knows that his time is short (Rev 12:12).

Peter, who remembered how he had fallen to Satan's temptation in his denial of the Lord, spoke from personal experience when he wrote:

> Your enemy the devil prowls around like a roaring lion looking for someone to devour (1 Pet 5:8).

What is the Christian's role?

In chapter 2 we saw that we are God's crack troops, his S.A.S. The ones who go into enemy-occupied territory and bring heaven to earth. We are in a strategic position:

we are in the world, but we are citizens of heaven (Phil 3:20). The world still lies in the control of Satan. Many Christians do not realize that, but Scripture is very clear:

> We know that we are children of God, and that the whole world is under the control of the evil one (1 Jn 5:19).

That was written *after* Christ's resurrection and ascension.

Satan is still 'prince of this world'. Our task is to get people out of the world ruled by Satan, in the sense that they are no longer a part of the world, and into the kingdom of God. To do that, of course, we have to remain in the world, yet not be conformed to it. No wonder then, in his great prayer at the very end of his ministry, Jesus asked his Father:

> My prayer is not that you take them out of the world but that you protect them from the evil one (Jn 17:15).

We saw that when Moses died, the archangel Michael did not rebuke Satan, because Satan was senior to him. But we, who belong to Christ, are no longer under Satan; we do not have to acknowledge his authority. We are living in the world, it is true, but we travel on a royal passport as a member of the kingdom of God. James says: 'Resist the devil, and he will flee from you' (Jas 4:7).

We are now God's chosen people, chosen to proclaim the victory of Christ. Chosen to set people free from bondage to Satan and his power, in the name of Jesus.

As we fight against injustice, poverty, hunger, want, immorality and vice, while we may well use every social and political means properly open to us, we know that we are not fighting only against human beings who cause

60

these things. We know that behind all these men there are spiritual forces of evil seeking to pollute, harm and destroy. We know the truth of Paul's words:

> For though we live in the world, we do not wage war as the world does. The weapons we fight with are not the weapons of the world. On the contrary, they have divine power to demolish strongholds (2 Cor 10:3–4).

Our weapons are prayer, fasting, faith, obedience and, above all, love. We are involved in spiritual warfare. We forget that at our peril. Never underestimate Satan's power. Personally, I do not ridicule him either; he is far more powerful than I am. But I go with the authority of the King of kings, at whose name every knee must bow, in heaven, on earth, and under the earth (Phil 2:10).

With this understanding of what is going on in the unseen but very real spiritual realm we are better equipped to engage in the battle. Others will see the tyrants and evil men who cause so much suffering and injustice in the world. Christians should recognize that there are principalities and powers working through these individuals in a similar way to that in which God longs to work through us. Similar but not identical, for our loving heavenly Father respects our individuality and our will; whereas Satan has no respect for those he uses. Once they have served his purpose, he discards and even disposes of them. Remember Judas Iscariot.

When we turn to prayer, as well as seeking the Father's blessing on people or nations, we may have to rebuke the powers of darkness. We are not to speak with them as we may speak with God; there is no question of holding a conversation with them. We proclaim the victory of Christ and command that they yield in his name. For instance, you may live in a house where the previous occupants were involved in particularly immoral practices or where there has been much sadness and tragedy. In such a situation I would pray something like this:

'I come in the name of Jesus Christ and take authority over any powers of darkness. In his name I command that you depart and I speak "peace" to this home and all who live here.'

In some cases such prayers are very necessary and I have gone from room to room speaking out similar words.

Sometimes I have felt particularly heavy and depressed. Experience has taught me that this often happens shortly before we enter what later proves to be a time of particular blessing. Very often, if only I remember to do it, a brief prayer rebuking the forces of darkness has caused the depression to lift immediately.

We shall be considering in later chapters what to pray for and how to do it, but that teaching will be all the more meaningful if you bear in mind the truths set out here. We face an enemy who is both evil and powerful. However, both he and his minions know already the final outcome—the victory is Christ's. When Jesus met the demonized man in the region of the Gadarenes, the spirits recognized him at once for who he was (it was men who didn't see):

'What do you want with us, Son of God?' they shouted. 'Have you come here to torture us before the appointed time?' (Mt 8:29).

It is my experience that they recognize those who belong to Christ as well. If we are also aware that there is an 'appointed time' for their destruction, we can proclaim that victory now and cause them to yield.

A word of warning

Over recent years there has been an increase in spiritism, experimenting with the ouija board, fortune telling and even witchcraft and black magic. It is becoming more common to meet people who have been involved in such dangerous practices and who have become contaminated in some way by their contact with evil powers. Christ's victory is sufficient to set these people free, but we need to know what we are about. It is sensible not to get involved in this particular form of deliverance ministry without help and guidance from someone with experience of it.

Also there are those who, having once had their eyes opened to the realities of the spiritual forces behind the scenes, can think of nothing else. Every sin, sickness and mental illness is due, in their eyes, to demonic influence. Beware that you do not go overboard in that way.

However, do not allow those warnings to cause you to hesitate to take up your post as a servant of God in an alien world. You can expect Satan to attack and test your faith but, provided you are abiding in Christ, he cannot touch you.

So let us be alert, and keep awake. Put on every item of God's armour. Many Christians in their time of prayer consciously put on every piece of that armour daily, picturing its purpose and effect. There is:

the belt of truth
the breastplate of righteousness
the shoes of the gospel of peace
the shield of faith
the helmet of salvation
the sword of the Spirit, the word of God
(Eph 6:14–17)

One final thing. Unconfessed sin leaves a chink in the armour. If we are engaged in bringing in the kingdom then we must ensure that we are no longer of the world ourselves. That would be like sitting on the very branch we are sawing off the tree!

5

In the Spirit and with the Spirit

Do you remember what Christ taught Nicodemus?

> Flesh gives birth to flesh, but the Spirit gives birth to spirit (Jn 3:6).

Paul amplifies that in his first letter to the Christians in Corinth when he explains that in our natural state, before we are born again of the Holy Spirit, we cannot receive spiritual truth or guidance. It doesn't make sense, it doesn't register with us, because a person must be spiritual in order to grasp spiritual things (1 Cor 2:14). There is a whole realm or area of life which a man cannot comprehend unless and until he is born of the Holy Spirit. Jesus told Nicodemus that until he is born again, a man cannot even see the kingdom of God, let alone enter it.

Let us relate this truth to what we have learnt about the way God is looking for a people to 'stand in the gap' in prayer.

God is Spirit (Jn 4:24). Originally he called creation into being by a word. God said, 'Let there be...' and there was. He has no physical hands or feet, but he chose to rule the material earth through man who is himself material. Man was created out of matter, the very dust of the earth. Man has a physical body. However, a man is not only body. God breathed his own life into man and, as he is Spirit, that gave man a spirit also. So God had created a living being on earth who was able to have spiritual communion with him. Man could receive God's orders or commands through his spirit and then carry them out through the use of his body. That is to say, he could physically control the earth because he could walk on it, dig it and generally do things to it. Thus God planned to have his will performed on earth by revealing it to man who was physically equipped to put it into effect.

We see this in Genesis 1:28, where man is instructed not only to populate the earth but to subdue it and exercise rule over every other creature. Similarly in Genesis 2:15 man is instructed to tend, guard and keep the earth. Genesis 3:8 implies that God was in regular communication with man, having an immediate, trusting relationship which, of course, was destroyed by man's sin of disobedience.

By referring to man's 'sin' I have immediately raised a new dimension. If man were only spirit (capable of receiving God's commands) and body (capable of carrying them out on a material earth) he would be little more than a robot. In fact, when God breathed his life into man, man became a living soul; capable of thinking, feeling and with a will which had the potential for independent expression and decision. In other words he had freedom of choice—of choosing to obey or disobey God. Freedom to remain as he was designed to be—the link between God's will in heaven and the fulfilment of that will on earth, or to make independent decisions according to his own thoughts or feelings.

In fact, God made it very clear to man that he was not to use his free will to make up his own mind about what was good and evil. So he was not to eat the fruit of the tree of the knowledge of good and evil. He was to rely on receiving, through his spirit, God's own knowledge of what was good, and gladly, joyfully, to obey that. God made it clear what he required, but he did not prevent man from exercising his free will independently. It was this which made man a living soul and not a robot. God's joy was to be that man, while free to reject him, would choose instead to love and obey him. Have you ever realized that you, a mere creature, can give joy to God by using your free will to say, 'Father, I give myself to you, to do your will, not my own'? We give joy to the Father when we follow the example of Jesus and say, as we have seen he said, 'A body you prepared for me.... I have come to do your will, O God' (Heb 10:5–7).

Perhaps I should mention that theologians differ as to whether man is bi-partite (body and soul/spirit) or tri-partite (body, soul, and spirit). I believe the latter view is the more scriptural—see 1 Thess 5:23 and Heb 4:12. The distinction is not crucial to the argument, provided the various functions of the soul and spirit are maintained. In any case, neither description should be pressed too far because man is a whole. The 'parts' of body, soul and spirit, which I separate for ease of understanding, in practice interrelate and overlap. So it is that we all know that worry in the mind can produce an ulcer in the stomach.

The soul in this explanation is 'me', the person I am; that which makes me 'me' and you 'you'; the person who thinks and feels and decides. God's original plan was for man to receive or learn of the divine will through his spirit and faithfully perform it through the use of his body. We can summarize the situation like this:

The body is world-conscious and embraces	hearing sight smell taste touch
The soul is self-conscious and embraces	emotion or feeling intellect or thinking will or deciding
The spirit is God-conscious and embraces	conscience intuition communion

This view of man is developed at length by Watchman Nee in his book *The Spiritual Man* (Christian Fellowship Publishers), though it would be unfair to attribute to him the particular application I am making here.

The definition is a little arbitrary because conscience and intuition can overlap with the soul. However, it is a working description because certainly God can and does communicate via conscience and intuition.

When man sinned, his 'life-line' to God was cut—causing the death God had warned would happen. His spirit withered and ceased to function in the way it was created to do. It seems that this 'withering' happened over a period because Adam's son, Cain, was still able to communicate with God (Gen 4). However, from then onwards there is no longer any general ability among men to communicate with God. In his mercy, God raised up an individual here and there and sent his Spirit upon him so that he could explain to the people God's plan and purpose. Even then, he left the nation free to choose whether they would obey or disobey. In the case of Jonah we see God having to cope with a prophet who was reluctant to fulfil his role, but the Almighty would not act to save the people of Nineveh without Jonah warning them of the judgement about to fall on them and their repenting and crying for mercy. Apart from these selected individuals who proclaimed the word of the Lord in each situation, man was no longer able to communicate with God because his spirit had ceased to function.

Because man was no longer able to receive his guidance from God, his soul (i.e. man himself) took its guidance from what it received through the senses of the body— sight, touch, etc. This fusion of body and soul became what the Bible calls 'flesh'. Man had indeed eaten of the tree of the knowledge of good and evil. He made up his own mind on what seemed to be good or evil according to what he saw or heard around him. Man, who had been put in charge of the earth and everything on it, was now misfunctioning and so the world was no longer governed according to God's will. No wonder Paul talks of the whole of creation groaning and being subject to frustration and decay; longing, as it were, for God's chosen sons to be revealed and for them to take up their rightful place (Rom 8:18–23).

Following the 'fall' therefore, we have man unable to receive guidance or light from God to direct him. In the fullness of time Christ, who is the Light to light every man (Jn 1:9), became man and, as man, used his free will to present himself as a pure and perfect channel to his Father to work his work through him. Conceived by the Holy Spirit, born of the Virgin Mary, he was indeed a second Man, the last Adam (1 Cor 15:45). His spirit was alive, his soul surrendered and his body available to God.

It is in this context that we can understand what Jesus means when he tells Nicodemus that what is born of the flesh is flesh, and only what is born of the Spirit is spirit. By our natural human birth we are only body and soul— 'flesh'. Our spirit is not functioning.

God revealed to Ezekiel what he planned to do (Ezek 36:25 ff). He said that first he would cleanse man from his sin. Then he would renew man's heart (the soul which had become fused with the body and was now 'flesh') and give him a new spirit capable of functioning as it should, a means of communication with its Creator. Man's hardness of heart would be softened ('flesh' in v 26 is contrasted with 'stone', not with 'spirit'). Then, when man's spirit was alive, there would be somewhere for the *Holy* Spirit to dwell. So God goes on to tell Ezekiel that he would put his own Spirit in man, encouraging and enabling him to walk obediently in God's ways.

This was fulfilled when Jesus came upon earth, redeemed us by his death and regenerated us by his resurrection. He has cleansed us who have responded from our sin. He has given us new, eternal life and made us a new creation (2 Cor 5:17). We have come alive in the spirit and the Holy Spirit has come to dwell in us alongside our own new spirit (Rom 8:16). Once again God has a means of ruling or ordering the earth through the willing co-operation of man. We can exercise lordship because, as Paul understood and explained, we have been raised up with Christ to sit with God in the heavenly realms (Eph 2:6). That is our heavenly ministry, so to speak; we can get into the throne room. In our earthly ministry we have his power, the power of the Holy Spirit who both communicates God's will and empowers us to carry it out. In the Old Testament, as we have seen, it was isolated individuals who were chosen and called to be God's mouthpiece. Prophets like Elijah, Isaiah, Jeremiah. It was one of the prophets, Joel, to whom God revealed that the time would come when he would pour out his Spirit on all his people, not just certain selected individuals (Joel 2:28 ff). That was fulfilled on the Day of Pentecost (Acts 2:16 ff). The power of the Holy Spirit is now available to every believer. Not every Christian believes this apparently, and not all who believe it appropriate it.

So the situation today is that God has not changed. He still wills to rule the earth through man. We, the redeemed, are now the body of Christ on earth. We have a live spirit to receive God's instructions into our minds and we can exercise our free will to choose to obey and offer our bodies for service. No longer are we to walk according to the guidance of the flesh (the fusion of body and soul)— we must put that to death. Instead, we are to walk by the Spirit, receiving our guidance from him.

Incidentally, we shall consider the practice of meditation in Chapter 10. Romans Chapter 8 provides an excellent source of material for several weeks.

Let's now return to a text that we have considered already, but in the context of this chapter it reveals a new light:

> I urge you, brothers, in view of God's mercy, to offer your *bodies* as living sacrifices, holy and pleasing to God—which is your *spiritual* worship. Do not conform any longer to the pattern of this world, but be transformed by the renewing of your *mind*. Then you will be able to test and approve what God's will is—his good, pleasing and perfect will (Rom 12:1–2).

Now we can relate all this to the matter of prayer.

Praying in the Spirit

Paul instructs us always to pray in the Spirit (Eph 6:18). What he means, of course, is that God knows very well what he longs to accomplish on earth. Instead of rushing in and praying for what we think is a good idea, which might be according to the 'flesh', we are to discover what

God's will is. We are to be directed by the Holy Spirit.

Sometimes we shall be very aware of a direct burden impressed upon us by the Spirit. At other times we may not be consciously aware of the Spirit's direction. However, we know that God's nature abides in us (1 Jn 3:9) and that we have the mind of Christ (1 Cor 2:16). So we may trust that as we mature and grow more Christlike the matters we feel burdened to pray for are, in fact, the burdens on God's heart also. We shall, as has been explained, be praying *in the Spirit.*

As our heart begins to beat in time with God's heart, we may find longings and burdens arising deep within us which we can hardly comprehend. They are stirrings in the depths of our spirits. They may spill over to our emotions. We know they are real but we cannot analyse them with our minds. Certainly we cannot formulate these longings into words. It is this experience to which Paul refers when he writes:

> In the same way, the Spirit helps us in our weakness. We do not know what we ought to pray, but the Spirit himself intercedes for us with groans that words cannot express (Rom 8:26).

I do not want to be dogmatic, but it seems to me that Paul is revealing an astonishing spiritual truth here which he develops in the next verse. Apparently, because God waits for man's co-operation before he brings in his will on earth, he sometimes meets the problem that man, even in his redeemed state, cannot comprehend just what that will is. Our finite minds cannot grasp the infinite wonder of God's plan. So, says Paul, God uses our willingness to 'pray down' his will, even when we cannot comprehend it; and the Holy Spirit, resident within us, will pray without our formulating words, in accordance with what *he* knows

God's will to be. Isn't that fantastic!

Certainly we are in deep water here, but we must accept that the truths of God are greater than our minds can grasp. To help us understand, Scripture will sometimes give us a description which will clarify one aspect of the total truth which, when laid alongside descriptions to explain another aspect, may seem difficult to reconcile. There are three statements about prayer which fall into the category, but each is true.

1. We have a right to enter the throne room boldly and with confidence to speak with our heavenly Father face to face (Heb 4:16).
2. Jesus is in heaven and is continually interceding for us at the Father's right hand (Heb 7:25–26).
3. The Holy Spirit also intercedes for us and all the saints, here on earth, with our own hearts (Rom 8:26–27).

There will be times, therefore, when we are praying with our minds, using words to express our thoughts. There will be times when we are praying without using words; the Holy Spirit will be interceding through us, interpreting what he knows to be God's will. We will feel the burden but not comprehend what it is. Both those experiences will be praying in the Spirit (capital 'S', meaning Holy Spirit).

However, Scripture teaches yet another manner of prayer: *with* the spirit (small 's' meaning our own spirit, given or brought to life when we are born again of the Holy Spirit).

Praying with the spirit

I will pray with my spirit, but I will also pray with my mind (1 Cor 14:15).

That translation from the New International Version makes it very clear what Paul means, by using the word 'my' instead of 'the' which is common among other versions. We can readily understand what Paul is referring to when he speaks of praying with his mind. As explained above, that is to use familiar words to express our thoughts. But what is praying with his spirit? From the context (1 Cor 14:2–25), particularly the previous verse (v 14), it is clear that he means praying in tongues. But what is that?

It is easier to understand if we use the phrase 'a different language' instead of 'tongues', for that is what it means; as in the phrase 'our mother tongue'—referring to the language of our native country. It is to use a language which the speaker has never learned and does not understand. It may be a language in use on earth in a different nation, as it was on the Day of Pentecost (Acts 2:4–11), or a heavenly language ('If I speak in the tongues of men *and of angels*' 1 Cor 13:1). It is a language given by the Holy Spirit but, once given, is then available for use by the one who receives it, as and when he or she decides to do so. It is entirely under the control of the speaker who may start and stop at will, as when he uses his native language. The place where this special language is 'stored', so to speak, is in the spirit and not in the mind. Hence Paul can talk of praying with his spirit (the gift language) or his mind (a language he has learned and understands).

What is its value?

Primarily, its value springs from the fact that it is a gift of God bestowed by the Holy Spirit. It also edifies, builds up the speaker (1 Cor 14:4).

The practical value is two-fold. First, we all know how rapidly we exhaust the human words of praise— 'Hallelujah', 'Praise him', 'Glory to God' and so on.

Even if there are others, we have to search our memory for them. How wonderful it is not to have to concentrate consciously on finding words. Instead we are free to devote our thoughts to God; his wonder, beauty, holiness and love. Yet the need to *express* our worship is met by using a language we do not have to think about or listen to or even understand. We just pour it out to God.

The second practical value of tongues is akin to the Holy Spirit interceding for us when we feel deep longings but cannot find words to express them. It is especially helpful also when praying against occult forces of darkness. Some verbal expression is needed, but we are not sure just what we are up against or what we should pray; but the Spirit does and he instructs our spirit.

What it is not

It is not some ecstatic utterance which overpowers the speaker. Nor is he sent into a trance. Anyone who disrupts a public gathering for worship with an unseemly use of tongues (and remember there is a seemly use) with the excuse 'I couldn't help it', does not understand the situation. The Holy Spirit may prompt or encourage him to speak out in tongues, but does not compel him to do so. It is the person's spirit which prays and by an act of will—which is part of his soul—he can control his spirit just as he can control his body. Paul spells this out with regard to the spiritual gift of prophecy, stating that the spirits of the prophets are subject to the control of prophets (1 Cor 14:32). He could have said exactly the same about those who speak in tongues because this is also a spiritual gift. In fact he clearly implies this by instructing that only two or at the most three people should speak in tongues at any one meeting, and they are to wait their turn. The person controls his spirit, his spirit must not control him.

Can all speak in tongues?

There is a difference of opinion among Christians about this. We must beware of thinking that those who disagree with our own view are not such good, sound or scriptural Christians as those who agree. The reason for the difference is that the Bible is not entirely clear.

Those who hold that not everyone may have the gift of tongues point to 1 Corinthians 12:30 where Paul asks if all speak in tongues. From the context it is clear that he expects and encourages the answer, 'No, they do not.' Alongside that, however, we must place 1 Corinthians 14:5 where Paul says he wants them all to speak in tongues. Which is rather pointless if it isn't possible anyway. An explanation which embraces both texts, without forcing the words to mean something Paul did not intend, is to make a distinction between speaking in tongues in public when the fellowship is gathered for communal worship, and doing so in our private prayers. Paul was certainly able to speak in tongues (1 Cor 14:18) but normally he preferred not to do so in public (v 19). For his personal prayers, as we have seen, he would pray both with his spirit and with his mind (1 Cor 14:15).

Experience would suggest that everyone who desires to pray in tongues may do so. That statement will be most frustrating for those who do so desire but have not yet done so. Certainly anyone who gets emotionally worked up (either for or against speaking in tongues) is unlikely to possess the gift. Those who are seeking this very lovely gift of the Holy Spirit should seek advice from mature Christians with experience in this field. On balance, it seems to be a case of 'all may—none must'.

It may be helpful to make the following brief comments. Understand that it is the *language* which is given, not the voice. You have to make your voice available by starting to make a sound. In the English language there are many more consonants than vowels, and the voice or tongue in our mouths is more used to using consonants. So why not begin by making a noise like 'nnn' or 'bbb...'? You don't have to shout, the Holy Spirit is gentle as a dove. You may feel very foolish to start with, but let me say again: the Holy Spirit provides the language, you provide the voice. That is why you always remain in control. I have discovered one rather strange fact: some people who have found it difficult to begin speaking in tongues have started by singing in tongues. Maybe it is because we are rather more used to humming or singing without words than we are to umming and arring. I am well aware of the fact that Satan can ape the gifts of the Spirit and people involved in the occult can sometimes 'speak in tongues'. On the rare occasions that I have heard them, I have found the sound unpleasant. There is a difference! But no Christian should allow that fact to hold him back from seeking all that God's Holy Spirit longs to give.

A final comment

There is a view which is less common today than a few years ago, that the gifts of the Holy Spirit, one of which is tongues, are not for today. They were given just to get the church started, so to speak. There is no scriptural warrant for such a view. Indeed Scripture makes it clear when these gifts will cease. The famous chapter on love (1 Cor 13) confirms that they are not eternal, but states that they will only be taken away when total perfection comes about (1 Cor 13:10). Then we shall know and understand fully even as now we are fully known and understood by God. There will be no need for gifts of healing then; no one will be sick. We shall not need a word of prophecy or of knowledge from the Lord then; for we shall be with him and see him as he is. That time has not yet come. Until it does these gifts are available. They are gifts from a loving heavenly Father to his children, to enable them to fulfil his will on earth.

Let Paul have the final word:

> Be eager to prophesy, and do not forbid speaking in tongues. But everything should be done in a fitting and orderly way (1 Cor 14:39–40).

6

The Faith Principle

What misunderstanding there is about faith! For years I have been confused about what we mean by having faith, exercising faith, holding on in faith. There are still areas of the subject which I do not fully understand, but I have certain broad principles clear in my mind; at least to my own satisfaction. So let me begin by clearing away some misconceptions.

First, faith is not some form of spiritual chit which we hand in to God to persuade him to reward us by giving us what we ask. Often I meet people who seem to have this understanding. They refuse to take medicines or have an operation, or they will not apply for financial aid from state social sources to which they are entitled, because they believe such action would reveal a lack of faith in God. Very occasionally God may make it clear to a particular person in a particular situation that in fact he does require that they accept no such aid from men; he will heal or provide directly. Usually, however, God will work through human resources. It seems to me that it is presumption rather than faith to ask God for his help and then lay down which channels he may or may not use in providing it. Nor is faith something we strive to stir up within us by some effort of will. Faith is simply the channel we open up to allow God's blessing and grace to flow.

Then again, there are people who will pray about a matter and then leave it to God to answer as he thinks fit. They may even begin or end their prayer with the words 'if it be thy will'. At first sight this appears to be very spiritual and, let me make it clear, sometimes that is indeed right. There are times when we just do not know what God's will is and we must leave it to him to act as he knows best. But that is not the most effective method of prayer.

I believe that most of us go through three stages as we mature in our Christian life. Initially we tend to give God instructions as though he were the genie of our magic lamp. 'God bless so and so, heal someone else, give me such and such.' As we grow in understanding we begin to realize that it is more important that God's will be done than our own. Our prayers change from instructions to requests which we would like to see answered, but we admit we may have got it wrong and add a phrase that God should act as he knows best. However, God wants to lead us to a more mature stage. Jesus treats us not only as servants but as friends. That is to say, he longs to share with us what the Father is doing. He wants us not only to pray 'your will be done' but to understand what that will is. Then, when we understand it, to pray for it. We saw this principle in the first chapter when we considered the words of Jesus about praying the Lord of the harvest to send labourers into the harvest. It is at that stage that the faith principle comes into action. Having understood what God desires; having prayed that he will do it; we then align ourselves with his will and act as channels of faith. It is our task to 'believe' God's plan into reality on earth. We know what God's plan is in a particular situation; we have asked him to fulfil it. Now we have to 'faith' it down from heaven to earth. Once again we are standing in the gap.

We see this principle at work constantly in the life of Jesus. We return to that text in Hebrews 10:5–7 where it is said of Christ that God had prepared a body for him and he had come to do his will. In his miracles Christ was acting as the channel through whom the Father worked his work. He knew what his Father wanted and he performed it in the faith it would happen.

Christ's teaching on believing prayer

This is explained most clearly in Mark 11 following the miracle of the fig tree. Jesus was hungry and, seeing a fig tree in leaf, he went to pick some fruit. However, the tree was barren so he cursed it. I used to feel for that tree, because the text clearly states that it wasn't the season for figs. Christ's action seemed so unfair. However, we have a fig tree in our garden and I now realize that the fruit forms at the end of the previous season. It is there all through the winter, long before the leaves show. If it wasn't the season for figs, it wasn't the season for leaves either. The tree Jesus saw was all show and no go! So Jesus simply commands that no one shall ever eat from that tree again. The following morning they pass along the same road and Peter notices that the tree has withered and comments on it, obviously surprised that Christ's words have had such an effect. Jesus then gives Peter a lesson about the place of faith in prayer. Most versions of the Bible record that Jesus said, 'Have faith in God,' but that is not the best translation. More exactly he said, 'Have God's faith,' that is, the faith *of* God.

What is God's faith? It is illustrated as early as the third verse of the Bible.

God said, 'Let there be light,' and there was light (Gen 1:3).

Isn't that simple? God said it: so it happened. To put it in human terms: once God had spoken, it never crossed his mind that it might not happen.

This principle of the link between the spoken word and the actual event which springs from it runs through the whole of Scripture. It is interesting to consider the use of the Hebrew word *dabar*. In the Old Testament Authorized Version it is translated 770 times as 'word' and 215 times as 'thing'. Perhaps the point I am making is most clearly illustrated in this verse:

> Not one thing hath failed of all the good things which the Lord your God spake concerning you; all are come to pass (Josh 23:14 av).

The word 'thing' in both cases is *dabar*. The thing spoken has become the thing accomplished or experienced in the lives of God's people.

When Jesus tells Peter, 'Have God's faith,' he is saying in effect, 'Are you surprised that I cursed the fig tree yesterday and it has withered today? Why? I spoke the *dabar* (word) and the *dabar* (thing) happened. You must adopt the same position of faith when you speak for God on earth.'

Jesus develops his point by giving an example of speaking to a mountain to move in the confident expectation that what is said will be done. That is to say, the speaker 'faiths' his word into becoming fact. The 'word' becomes 'flesh', so to speak.

Finally Jesus explains the principle behind it all in verse 24. Most versions of the Bible translate this along the lines, 'Whatever you pray for, believe you receive it and you will.' In fact a more accurate translation is—'Believe that you *did* receive it, and you will.' What Christ is teaching is that if we are in line with God's will then, of course, we have only to ask and it will be done immediately by God in heaven. But it is up to us who believe to get the answer spoken in heaven made real here on earth. We do that by opening a channel from heaven to earth for it to flow down. That channel is our faith. We *believe* the answer into being. Incidentally 'faith' and 'belief' are virtually interchangeable; they both translate one word in the original.

If you find this principle difficult to take in, you may find it helpful to use your time of meditation drawing out the meaning of the following texts: John 15:7; 16:23–4; and 1 John 5:14–15.

The most obvious illustration of the faith principle in the Old Testament is the story of Elijah in 1 Kings 18. God had sent a drought on the land. After three years God tells Elijah that he is about to send rain. That is to say he has let Elijah into his confidence and revealed his will to him. Then there is the contest between the priests of Baal and Elijah on Mount Carmel which ends with the slaughter of the priests and the acknowledgement of the people that Jehovah is God. Following this, Elijah climbs to the top of Carmel and bends down to the ground with his face between his knees. It does not say he was praying; perhaps he was. I am certain, however, that he was engaged in *believing* prayer. He knew God's will; he believed it had already been done, the word spoken, in heaven. He was 'faithing' it into reality on earth. He sends his servant to look towards the sea. He returns to report that there is nothing. Elijah sends him again. Still there is nothing. Seven times that happens. It is only recently that I have noticed Scripture says Elijah was on the top of the mountain. For years I thought he was at the bottom and the poor old servant was sent to climb it seven times in one day—which might have put something of a strain on the relationship between them. I can imagine Elijah hearing the report from his servant and saying to God, 'But you have promised. I *know* the rain is coming. This is your will. I proclaim it on earth. You have given it, I receive it.'

How soon do you give up? When you pray and you do not see the answer at once, do you assume God hasn't heard? Remember what we learned from Daniel who could not understand a divine revelation he had been given and prayed for the interpretation. It was three weeks before he had the vision of the angel who gave the explanation. The delay was caused by opposition in the heavenly realm. I do not know what caused the delay in the case of Elijah and the rain, but the prophet would not give up. He *knew* God was going to send rain and he waited there on Mount Carmel until it came; faithing it down on the strength of God's word. Seven times he sent his servant. What would have happened had it not come then? I am sure he would have sent him an eighth time, a tenth time, a twentieth time. God had *said*, so Elijah had God's faith it must happen. At the seventh time the servant reports that there is a very tiny cloud, the size of a man's hand, rising out on the sea. 'That's it, that's it; here it comes. That's what I've been waiting for. Go down and warn Ahab to get back home before the rain stops him.' It was only a tiny cloud, but faith was easier now, with that, than when there was nothing. But faith had brought that cloud into being in the first place.

Of course, it is easy to see the faith principle at work in a prophet like Elijah. It is a different matter when we are called to put it into operation ourselves. We must beware of presumption. God is sovereign; we are not. It is *his* will we faith into being, not ours. Elijah knew it was God's will to send rain, it wasn't his own idea. How careful we must be in our desire to exercise faith that we do not impose our own hopes and wishes on God, nor put pressure on those around us by telling them this or that is God's will, and they must 'believe' with us.

This is a very difficult area and I do not pretend I have learned how to handle it. I am simply sharing what I believe Scripture teaches and pressing on to discover how I can make what God promises real in my own experience. So often I am tempted to water down God's promises to fit my experience. Whereas the teaching of Christ about faith would stretch our experience until it reaches his promises.

Even so, we must take care how we do that. I am uneasy when someone uses this principle to try to force someone to believe he is healed when patently he is not. I understand the motive behind it. It is to encourage the sick person to have faith. 'You have prayed for your healing, so believe you have received it—you are healed!' That is the reasoning, but it seems to me that this goes beyond what Christ actually taught. 'Believe you did receive it and you will,' is not quite the same as, 'Believe you did receive it and you have.'

To me the situation is more akin to a son asking his father to help him out of some financial difficulty. The father agrees and tells his son that he has made a credit transfer to the son's account. In one sense the son has received it, it is in his account; but he still has to draw the money out before he has the benefit of it. If we believe our healing is in accord with God's will then, having prayed for it, we should believe we have received it from our heavenly Father. We then have to faith it into being. Maybe it will be instantaneous, maybe it will come over a period beginning with a sign of improvement as tiny as a cloud the size of a man's hand. But that small improvement is to be the first rung of the ladder on which we stand to increase our faith for the next rung.

What is faith?

The author of the letter to the Hebrews defines it this way:

> Faith is the substance of things hoped for, the evidence of things not seen (Heb 11:1 AV).

The word 'substance' is the one used by him in Hebrews 1:3 where Jesus is described as the exact representation of God's essential *being, nature* or *person*. The meaning is that faith accepts and receives now something that will happen in the future. Suppose you want to attend some event like the Olympic Games. You apply for a ticket and it arrives. If someone says to you, 'I hope you will get in,' you will say, 'But I will! I have my ticket with a seat number on it.' The ticket turns a wish into reality. It is a substance, something you actually have in your hand. Faith operates in the present tense: it receives what it will obtain. It says, 'Amen, it is done.'

Does that mean, therefore, that we should never pray for anything more than once? That cannot be so. Jesus told two stories to encourage us to persist in prayer—the friend at midnight (Lk 11:5 ff) and the widow and unjust judge (Lk 18:1 ff). Admittedly, in those stories, both the friend and widow persisted only until they received the answer they sought. After that there was no further need to continue. What is the situation if we believe our prayer has indeed been granted in heaven but we have not yet received it on earth? It seems to me that we are justified in reminding God of his promises. We may even feel it is appropriate to thank him for his answer while we wait for it to be made real. Elijah was surely doing *something* while his servant was going back and forth looking for the rain. Surely there is such a thing as a believing or faith-building prayer.

Praying within the area of our faith

Sometimes we may pray for a situation which, from a human point of view, seems impossible to solve. But that is exactly what it is—from a human point of view. That is why Paul reminds us we walk by faith, not by sight (2 Cor 5:7). Very often the appearance of things breeds doubt and fear. We see someone who is ravaged by disease and, while we look at them, we know we cannot pray in faith. We are influenced so strongly by what we see. That is why the writer to the Hebrews tells us that faith is the evidence of things *not* seen.

A moment's thought will show us that we can only pray believing prayer within the area of our faith. We need to ask ourselves, 'What do I have faith for?' If we pray, 'Lord, convert my next-door neighbour,' and leave it at that, we are not truly standing in the gap faithing our prayer into being. Do we really expect it to happen? If in all honesty we cannot say we believe it, then we need to reduce our prayer to proportions for which we do have faith. Do you dare to believe that, if you ask him, God will give you an opportunity to talk to your neighbour about what Christ means to you, within the next two weeks? If so, then pray for that and faith it into being. When you have received that, perhaps you will have faith to pray for an opportunity to invite your neighbour to a special meeting and that he will accept.

In this way we can build up our faith expectancy. So often we jump in at the deep end. Start small and increase the area of your faith as you see results. Many who cannot honestly pray against a cancer believingly may be able to pray with assurance that someone's headache will be gone within two hours. I am not suggesting that you ought not to pray against a cancer or anything else until you can do so with utter confidence that you have received your petition. However, that should be your aim as you continue to mature in the faith. James says:

> The prayer offered in faith will make the sick person well; the Lord will raise him up (Jas 5:15).

What about failure?

In my own experience there have been times when, so far as I can judge, I really have had faith for something but it has not happened. I must be honest about this. It does no honour to God to pretend or make excuses. I can do one of two things. I can say that I have misunderstood Scripture or even that it is not true. That all that I have said in this chapter, although it is utterly scriptural so I believe, is incorrect. That we are *not* to believe that when we have prayed for something, we have received it and we will. Or I can say that the principle is correct but somewhere along the line something has gone wrong. Perhaps I was at fault, or some other factor unknown to me came into play. I go back to that prayer of Daniel where the forces of wickedness in the heavenly sphere delayed the answer for three weeks. Never forget we are in a spiritual war. It really is the biggest battle in eternity. It is between the kingdom of darkness and the kingdom of light. To win it cost the life of the Son of God. The outcome is now certain and sure, but it is not yet fully realized on earth. Meanwhile, as we have seen, Satan is thrashing out doing all the hurt and damage on earth that he can because only a short time is left to him (Rev 12:12).

In a war you do not necessarily win every individual battle. There are casualties. I realize that during his own earthly ministry Christ did win every fight against Satan. I also understand that the same power of the Holy Spirit who was in Christ has been given to dwell in us and we are to do at least the same things that he did (Jn 14:12). However, I have not yet attained to this high calling. Nevertheless, like Paul, I will put behind me my past failures and press on to the goal set before me (Phil 3:12–14). The practice of faith, like anything else worth having, has to be learned. We do not sit down at the piano for the first time and expect to play a Beethoven Sonata. Why do we assume that we can exercise the faith of God himself in all its fullness immediately?

Of course I know how difficult it is, if we have prayed in faith for someone's healing and they have died, to find faith to pray for the next sick person who comes to us. Nor does it answer the problem to say that death itself is the perfect healing: I know that and believe it. But that is not what Christ meant when he sent the disciples out to heal the sick. Nevertheless, I am convinced, utterly convinced deep within me, that this is the way Christ is leading his church. Our failures are to make no difference. We are to go on practising the faith of God. I do not fully understand but I am sure this is the way through. After all, every cook who bakes a cake experiences an occasional failure. She may not recall what ingredient she left out or what went wrong. But it doesn't prevent her believing she can bake a perfectly good cake on the next occasion. So with us: our faith is finally to be in God himself, not in the answer we do or do not receive.

It is always easier to pull down than to build up. That is why Paul and the other writers tell us so frequently in their letters to encourage one another, build each other up. If you have ever attended a meeting led by someone with a genuine Christian healing ministry you will notice that usually he first expounds Scripture explaining God's promises. He may well invite testimonies from people who have been healed in the past. This is not to create a false emotionalism but an atmosphere of expectant faith.

Remember that even Jesus himself was hindered in working miracles in his own home town because of the people's lack of faith (Mt 13:58).

So do not fear failure. Faith involves the risk of not succeeding. Above all, do not feel guilty. If I allowed Satan to cripple me by convicting me of guilt every time I have failed to receive the answer to my prayer, I could never function as a minister of the kingdom. Mind you, I am not content to stay there in my failure. I am going to press on until I break through into that area which I am convinced is there, where my prayers are answered regularly. Where I do know what God's will is; where I do believe I have received the answer, and where I regularly see it realized before my eyes.

7

Petition and Intercession

At last we come to that aspect of prayer which more than any other reflects God's call to us to stand in the gap. Both petition and intercession involve asking: petition is for ourselves, intercession is for others.

Petition

Some people adopt a false humility and will not ask for their own needs to be met. It is false because it is not humility at all. It is fear based on lack of self-worth. They do not really believe that they are important to God; certainly they cannot have entered into the 'Abba—Father' relationship which Paul wrote about in Romans 8:15, to which we referred in Chapter 2. This attitude is actually sinful because such people belittle Christ's sacrifice on the cross. He thought they were worth dying for but, apparently, their own opinion is that he made a mistake. In fact their value is the price God was willing to pay to have them for himself. Of course we were sinners. I admit that if I were someone else looking at me, I would not be willing to give my life for the person I was. But Christ's love is so great that even while I was still such a sinner he died for me (Rom 5:7–10). Paul uses this argument to illustrate that God does desire to give us all we need and more:

> He who did not spare his own Son, but gave him up for us all—how will he not also, along with him, graciously give us all things (Rom 8:32).

God longs to give us all things; not only our material needs but health and peace and joy.

I have even heard someone say that they did not like to bother God with their needs when he had so many world-shattering problems to deal with. That attitude would be laughable if it were not so sad. What an inadequate idea that reveals of just who God is. He is not man who is capable of concentrating on only one thing at a time. He can give each of us his full attention all the time. He is *God*! He has much more time to share himself with us than we make available to share ourselves with him.

God delights when we ask him to meet our needs. Think how much it would grieve a human father to discover his son was living in poverty and seeking help elsewhere, before asking him. God is our heavenly Father who has infinite resources. How it must sadden him if we do not ask, and simply try to manage on our own or go elsewhere for help.

When the disciples asked Christ to teach them to pray he specifically included petition: 'Give us this day our daily bread.' We not only have a right to ask God for the things we need, it is disobedience not to do so. In my own family we have brought anything and everything we need to the Lord. I was ordained older than many men. At thirty-five I had a growing family. As a new curate, my salary was just under half what I had been earning in business and we had to watch our pennies. My wife would pray before going into the butcher's shop that she would pick the most economical joint. Someone once commented that this might prove to be selfish because someone else might need it more than we did—but of course they were as free to pray for their needs to be met as we were for ours.

Obviously, it is wrong to ask from wrong motives or to use what we seek on our lusts (Jas 4:3–4). However, Jesus clearly taught that if we human parents like to give good things to our children, even more does our heavenly Father long to give them to those who ask him (Mt 7:7–11). It is right that we should seek his will for our lives rather than our own, but the two are not always destined to be different. His desire is that we should be full of joy, and while we must want him for himself rather than for what he gives us, he delights to surprise us with all sorts of good and enjoyable gifts. The Christian is not to be a deprived person, but one living in abundance. Remember, however, that our life does not consist of material possessions.

Intercession

Paul tells us that God 'has blessed us in the heavenly realms with every spiritual blessing in Christ' (Eph 1:3). That is to say, the whole storehouse of heaven is open to us. We live in the world. In Christ's 'high-priestly' prayer immediately before he was betrayed, which is recorded for us in John 17, he specifically said he was not asking his Father to take his disciples out of the world (v 15). It was essential to God's plan that he should have someone in the world to earth his will. We, today, are God's people in the world, but we have access to the storehouse of every spiritual blessing in the heavenly places. Our intercessory prayer is essential to God. He is only waiting, but he *is* waiting, for his own to cry to him and he will open that storehouse and pour out all we seek. However, I have come to understand that there is a particular attitude we need to adopt in intercession which does not apply to other aspects of prayer.

I constantly use my imagination and I have always pictured myself when I pray, as coming before the throne and facing God, so to speak: looking towards him. This attitude is surely right when we make our confession or bow before him in adoration, praise and thanksgiving. It also has a place, initially, with regard to intercession. We need to come before him as we present our petitions and share with him as we seek to discover his will. However, once we are in the position of understanding what his will is and believing we have received our petition then, to use picture language, we have to turn so that we stand alongside God and face towards the object of our prayers. From this position we proclaim or command that what we have requested (and obtained) be fulfilled, made real, on earth. I suppose that this final stage might not be 'prayer' as we usually understand it. Nevertheless I am now convinced that our work of intercession is not complete without it. In his ministry Jesus both taught and illustrated this principle.

With regard to his teaching, we find this in his instructions about prayer following the incident of the fig tree we were considering in the previous chapter. Jesus refers to *speaking* to the mountain to be moved. The principle is even more clearly explained in the passage where, after stating that Peter is the rock on which he will build his church, he goes on to say that whatever Peter binds on earth will be bound in heaven and whatever he looses on earth will be loosed in heaven (Mt 16:19). Incidentally, this promise is repeated in Matthew 18:18, where it is not limited to Peter alone. In both instances there is a very unusual construction in the Greek which most translations do not reflect. The tense of the verb is not a simple future, the past is involved also. It is as though Christ is wanting to avoid stating that heaven simply endorses what the disciples do on earth. Rather, they will be acting in accord with what has already been done in heaven. That is to say, what they bind on earth *will have been bound* in heaven. This teaching runs alongside that recorded in John 20: 22–23, where the risen Christ breathes on his disciples and commands that they receive the Holy Spirit. He then tells them that if they forgive anyone's sins they are forgiven and if they do not forgive them they are not forgiven. Here the implication is clearly that they will be guided by the Holy Spirit. It seems to me that it is all of a piece with what I have been seeking to explain throughout this book. God has his will in heaven; we are to discover that will; then we are to ask that it be done; after that we are to believe we have received it; finally we are by faith to proclaim it into being.

The most vivid example of this principle is the description of the raising of Lazarus from the dead recorded in John 11. First, from verse 4, we know that Jesus understood the will and plan of his Father in the situation. It was for God's glory so that Jesus himself might receive glory through it. Secondly, when he comes to the tomb (v 41) he speaks first to God. The record even gives the detail that he lifted up his eyes. That is to say, spiritually he took his eyes off the situation and faced towards his Father. The actual words recorded are not a request for Lazarus to be raised; rather they clearly imply that Jesus had already asked for this. He thanks his Father that he has heard him. That is to say, that he has already received what he has asked for. He even explains that he is speaking out publicly for the very purpose of making it a teaching example for the benefit of the onlookers (vv. 41–42). Finally, Jesus turns from talking to his Father and faces the object of his prayer—Lazarus in the tomb—and commands that what he has already received come to pass:

'Lazarus, come out'... and he does (vv. 43–44).

Although this is a particularly vivid example of the principle involved, it was not something new. We see it operating in the Old Testament in Exodus 17:8–16. The people of Israel were attacked by the Amalekites. Moses stood on a hill-top overlooking the battle with the rod of God in his hand. While his hands were raised Israel prevailed, but if he lowered them the Amalekites gained the advantage. As Moses grew weary Aaron and Hur held up his arms until Israel finally won the battle. This incident could not illustrate more clearly God's plan to use man in the bringing of his will upon earth. If man does not stand in the gap, or if he grows weary, the enemy prevails. There is no record that Moses prayed on that occasion, although it seems probable that he did. What is clear is that the end result was that Moses was aware that he had been given authority to bring in the will of God that his people should win the battle. He used that authority not by praying towards God but by looking in the same direction as God, towards the situation.

So often when we intercede we put God between us and the need. We pray to him and ask him to act for us. Whereas God desires that once we have understood what his will is, we stand between him and the need. That is to say, he asks us to act for him. We ask him to heal the sick, whereas he says, '*You* heal them, by my power in you.' He sent his disciples out to preach the kingdom and to heal the sick (Lk 9:2); he did not say, 'Ask *me* to preach and ask *me* to heal.' The power is his and he must have all the glory but, as I have been stressing, that power is in us. God works on earth through man.

> ...who is able to do immeasurably more than all we ask or imagine, according to *his power that is at work within us* (Eph 3:20).

Do not worry if you cannot always differentiate between the power of the Holy Spirit and the power of the risen Christ. Scripture does not always differentiate either. But do hold to the truth that we are intended to be power-full people. So when you intercede, as well as praying to God, imagine the situation you are praying about and direct his power upon it in your mind's eye. It is as though you are holding a hose-pipe directing life-giving water onto the situation, or operating the spotlight of Christ upon it. You are not the source of the power, that is of God; but he allows us the privilege of giving that power direction. Come boldly in the name of Jesus and command the powers of darkness to give way.

Sometimes it will be possible to do this literally. You may be praying for someone's healing and you will be able to lay on hands as you pray. Then it is very easy to direct the power of God upon them when the object of your prayer is physically present with you. But the principle holds good in other situations also. As you pray, imagine the answer actually happening. 'See' the sick person bathed in light, with healing pouring into his body; see him rising up restored. In your mind 'cut' the bonds which bind people or nations. As you do this, however, do not try to summon up some power from within yourself; that would be to enter the realms of magic or even the occult. Simply see yourself as the channel God is using to convey *his* power from heaven to earth. Speak with authority, God's authority. Use the name of Christ. He has given us the right to use it, and at his name every knee must bow—not only every human knee but beings in the spiritual realm also (Phil 2:10).

Let me repeat the truth I have come to understand. God is looking for somewhere to get into this world he has created. He found that most perfectly in Jesus Christ, but he finds it also in all who love Jesus and obey him. To such

97

the Father will come with his Son and will actually dwell within them (Jn 14:23). As we offer our bodies as a living sacrifice, he will dwell in us and by his Holy Spirit he will work his work through us as he did through Christ when he was on earth.

To put it bluntly, God is delighted if we almost pester him with prayer, crying to him earnestly in travail until we prevail. This is not because he is reluctant to grant us what we ask, but because he wants to bring us to the stage where we desire to see his will done on earth as much as he desires it.

Several years ago one of my relatives gave birth to twins. As sometimes happens, they were premature and there was concern about their survival. When the news came through I went to my room to say a prayer for them. That phrase just about sums it up; I said a prayer. As I left the room, it suddenly hit me what my cousin must be going through, waiting and watching. I returned to prayer, reminding God that these were two precious lives; telling him how long they had been carried in the womb and pleading with him to bring them through the crisis to a full life. As I came to the end of my prayer I felt the Lord say to me, 'Now you are just beginning to experience a little of what I have been feeling for them all the time.' They did survive. No doubt many others in the family had been praying also. I don't know if they learned the same lesson about the heart of God and the place and power of intercession.

Intercession may prove to be a very costly prayer. We may have to open ourselves until we can imagine and even feel the hurt or anguish of both the heart of God and of the person for whom we pray. It can also bring great reward when we hear, perhaps much later, of the direct result of our prayers. Perhaps we shall not hear, this side of the resurrection, what much of our intercession does accomplish. It may be that God will use you to pull down an evil government in some distant nation, not with bombs but by storming heaven with your prayers and then speaking out on earth, from your place of prayer, the answer already granted in heaven.

Fasting

If, as I believe, very little practical teaching about prayer is given in our churches, teaching about fasting must be almost non-existent. Yet our Lord not only set an example by fasting himself, he instructed his followers to do so also. In Matthew 6, which is part of the sermon on the mount, Jesus teaches his disciples about giving to the needy (vv. 1–4), about prayer (vv. 5–14) and about fasting (vv. 16–18). In each case he says '*when* you give', '*when* you pray', '*when* you fast'. These are not options which the Christian may adopt if he feels so inclined, they are part and parcel of what it means to be a follower of Christ. To him fasting is as much involved in being a disciple, as giving and praying. My difficulty is that it is a subject which deserves far more space than I can give it here, yet by including it only at the end of a chapter on intercession I may give the impression that it isn't really very important. I am coming to realize it is far more important in our ministry of prayer than I have recognized in the past.

What is the purpose of fasting? Certainly it is not to twist God's arm, so to speak. When an athlete goes into training he does not do it to impress the judge or umpire that he takes his running seriously; he does it to improve his own performance. So it is with our spiritual life. We fast because of the spiritual benefit it is to us, not to impress God.

We have seen already that following man's disobedience in the garden of Eden he became 'flesh', his body controlled his soul. The Christian has been born again of the Holy Spirit and we are now to take our guidance and direction from the Spirit, through our own spirit. Paul instructs:

> Clothe yourselves with the Lord Jesus Christ, and do not think about how to gratify the desires of the sinful nature [the flesh] (Rom 13:14).

Paul knew only too well the pull of that old nature and explained:

> I beat my body and make it my slave so that after I have preached to others, I myself will not be disqualified (1 Cor 9:27).

The word translated 'beat' is literally 'give it a black eye'. Paul is determined to rule his body; it does not rule him. Fasting is an excellent and, I believe, a necessary discipline to keep the body in its place as servant of the soul, not its master. It is not enough to say 'I am not overweight' or 'I do not eat too much'. This is to do with spiritual discipline. I like good food and my wife is a good cook. The very fact that I find it difficult to fast shows what a hold food has over me. Scripture is very clear that there is a continual battle between the flesh and the Spirit (Gal 5:16–25). There are two ways in which we can allow the Spirit to have the victory in our lives day by day. One is deliberately to follow the way of the Spirit; set ourselves to know and obey his direction. The other is to crucify the flesh with its passions and desires (Gal 5:24–25). That is to say, increase the one and reduce the other. Fasting is part of the work of crucifixion of the flesh. By breaking its power over us we open ourselves more to the Holy Spirit. Scripture teaches that there is a place for both feasting and fasting.

I must admit that I have not experienced lengthy fasting; the longest total fast I have undertaken has been of forty-eight hours, and that was of food only—I continued to take liquids. In my own fellowship I have, for many years, missed out the meal immediately prior to a service at which I am to preach. If I know I am to engage in some particular form of deliverance ministry, I will fast beforehand, and also on other occasions when there is a particular burden for prayer. While I believe that all Christians are to intercede, there are some with a particular calling as intercessors—in fact I believe they are God's gifts to his church as much as healers, teachers, prophets etc. These intercessors will frequently fast for days at a time, possibly having one light meal each evening during the period. Let me stress, however, that the fact that God calls some to this particular ministry does not mean that the rest of us are released from the need either to pray or to fast.

There are certain illnesses which may prevent a person from fasting. Diabetes is an obvious example. Expectant and nursing mothers should probably not fast either. Coffee and tea drinkers may suffer caffeine withdrawal symptoms if they give up these beverages suddenly. In my own case, I was so surprised at the effect when I stopped coffee and tea—a niggling headache and feeling utterly grotty for thirty-six hours—that I have not gone back onto them. I had not realized I was so addicted.

I have not found many books on this subject, but I can commend two: *God's Chosen Fast* by Arthur Wallis, (Kingsway Publications); and *Shaping History Through Prayer and Fasting* by Derek Prince, published by Fleming H. Revell.

If this is an area of discipleship you have not yet explored, let me repeat; fasting is not an optional extra for some, it is a discipline which Christ assumed all his followers would practise.

8

The Where, the When and the How

Every Christian, or every Christian I have met and talked with on the subject, agrees that we ought to pray. Of course, Scripture confirms this:

> They should always pray and not give up (Lk 18:1).
> Pray continually (1 Thess 5:17).
> You do not have, because you do not ask God (Jas 4:2).

The trouble is that while we agree we ought to pray, we don't do it. We are very good at deceiving ourselves. We may make resolutions that we really will be more disciplined about this. We may 'have our quiet time' when we study the Scriptures with the aid of some Bible notes and end with a quick prayer or two based on the passage we have just read. But as for 'standing in the gap', calling down God's will on earth, we haven't even reached the starting line. But should someone ask us if we pray or how long we pray, we confidently assure them we do and tell them the total period of our quiet time, as though that was prayer. Now, meditating on Scripture is an important part of the time we set aside for prayer. It has to do with our coming to the throne and spending time with our heavenly Father, discovering his will. But it is not itself prayer in the fullest sense.

I am told that some time ago a survey was made among Christians in America to discover how long they spent each day in actual prayer. The average worked out at one minute. They then conducted a similar survey among ministers. As you would expect it was more; much more; double, in fact: two minutes! I have no means of checking the truth of that information and it would not be worth quoting it except that, when I heard it, it made me think just how long I myself spent each day in actual prayer. It was longer than the result in the survey (remember that was the average), but not as long as I had fondly imagined. May I suggest that you stop and calculate honestly how long you spend in prayer each day? Then ask yourself if that is satisfactory—in your own eyes, let alone God's.

The problem is very simple—*it is difficult*! Difficult to make time to pray: difficult to find a place to pray: and then, if we have managed that, praying itself is difficult. Jesus himself knew those difficulties; certainly about time and place. He was in such demand with the crowds following him everywhere. Often he had to go up a mountain or into a garden and that had to be at night or early in the morning, to make a time and a place for prayer.

> Very early in the morning, while it was still dark, Jesus got up, left the house and went off to a solitary place, where he prayed (Mk 1:35).

If you mean business with God, you need to make time to pray and to find a place to pray. Occasionally someone will point out that Jesus did not have a regular time or place for prayer and so we do not need that either—it is too legalistic. Usually such people conveniently forget that Jesus began his ministry with a forty-day fast in the wilderness! We need to remember that Jesus spent every moment of his life, except one horrific experience while he hung on the cross, in a conscious, unbroken relationship with his Father. Surely none of us would claim to have that. If *he* felt the need for a definite time and place for prayer, how much more essential it is for us.

You may notice that I refer to *finding* a place but *making* time. In my experience I do not find time to pray, I have to make it. If I do not set a time and guard it jealously, then it is gone. Let me just say that I try not to be legalistic about it. If I am called out to some need or emergency, I go; and I don't spend the rest of the day thinking, 'I haven't had my prayer time so God won't bless me today.' But if I found that such calls arose frequently during my prayer time then I would change my prayer time.

The time we make will be different for each person. For many of us, I believe for most of us, the best time is before the business of the day begins. I like to start the day with God. There may be a few who genuinely find that the evening is best. My guess is that these people will need to be particularly disciplined. It is so easy just to finish off the sewing, the painting, the study—or just see the end of the programme on television—and give God the fag end of the day when they are tired.

It may be a different time for different members of the family. When our children were young babies, before I was ordained and when I had a job in the city, I used to get up when they woke for their early morning feed. For a mother, it may be when her husband has gone to work and the children off to school (but what do you plan for the school holidays?). Circumstances change. I have altered my prayer time to fit the different situations as the children have grown up. With regard to finding a place, for some it may be very difficult indeed. Nowadays I am fortunate, I have my study. Many use their bedroom. But what if you share a bedroom—especially if you are the only Christian in your family? Maybe you will have to set off early for work or college and call in at a local church. I know of one person who travels to London each day by train. He spends the forty-five minute journey praying. I admire him, but it is not something I can do; my thoughts are too easily distracted.

Perhaps in what I have said above about making a time and finding a place for prayer, I have not covered your particular circumstances and you want to say, 'In my case it is just impossible.' Well, only you know your situation. However, having a time and a place is so important that I feel I must set out one or two facts.

We always find time to do the things that are most important to us.

We do, you know. Oh there is never time to do all the things we would *like* to do (unless we are housebound). It is a matter of priorities and it may be we need to put prayer higher up the list.

It takes time to get to know someone.

One of the major causes of marriage breakdown is lack of communication. Husband and wife have lost the ability, if they ever had it, of telling each other what they think or feel. If they do try, the other partner doesn't really hear what is said. It is true of all relationships that there needs to be communication. You cannot get to know God unless you spend time with him, sharing your thoughts and listening to his. The problem is not on his side—he has set aside eternity for you.

Time spent in prayer saves time.

I do not understand why this is so; it is a spiritual, not a natural law. A great woman of prayer once said, 'I spend three hours a day in prayer, unless I am very busy—when I spend four.' God does not often speak to me directly. By that I do not mean the gentle but insistent prompting of the Holy Spirit within my spirit, but occasions when I have actually heard words within my mind, even to the tone of voice. I remember one occasion when I was very busy, with a hundred and one things to do that day. I recall I came to my prayer time with a completely wrong attitude. I dashed to my study with my mind on the things I had to do, regarding prayer as a necessary chore to be got through as quickly as possible. In this most unspiritual state, as I began to 'say my prayers', a voice broke through in my mind and said very clearly but gently, 'Where, in Scripture, does it say I ran anywhere?' It was so totally unconnected with anything I was thinking and such an unusual question, that I have no doubt it was the Lord. As far as I know, no one had ever pointed that out to me, but I now realize that it is true. There are instances in Scripture when people run to Jesus but none, that I can find, when he ran to them. Jesus always had time. That slowed me down for that day. I frequently forget that truth but it is a fact in my experience that time spent in prayer does not reduce the time available for the things I have to do. The things I have to do don't seem to take so much time if I have prayed.

We grow like the people we spend time with.

In our family we used often to laugh (kindly, I hope) about people who seemed to grow to look like the dog they had as a pet. Or maybe the dog grew like them! That may have been imagination, but it is certainly true among people. We pick up mannerisms, expressions and phrases from others. How often we hear someone say 'He does remind me of his father'? How wonderful if people said exactly that of us as Christians! 'They do remind me of

106

their heavenly Father.' But that will only happen as we almost subconsciously pick up God's attitudes, thoughts and will, as we spend time with him.

Consider the influences upon us. How do you spend your day? Assume we spend eight hours sleeping; then eight hours working, two travelling, one or two over meals, possibly in the company of others or reading the paper, two watching television or listening to the radio. That is thirteen or fourteen hours out of the day receiving impressions and absorbing teaching or attitudes from the world. But we Christians are the ones who are to influence the world rather than be influenced by it. Scripture puts it stronger; we are to reign or have the dominion over the world as God's stewards. If we are not to be conformed to the world and its ways, we must set aside time for the Holy Spirit to transform us by the renewal of our minds in the ways of God.

We are creatures of habit.

We feel more relaxed in familiar surroundings. Have you ever been in a supermarket where they have rearranged the lay-out? You will find all the housewives retracing their steps in frustration because the items they want are not in the familiar place. If we make a time and find a place for prayer we will find a security in the familiarity we sense each day. We will be able to relax and concentrate on God more quickly.

The secret of it all is simply this: be flexible, but be organized.

How to pray

We learn to pray by doing it. You cannot learn to swim unless you are in the water—however much instruction you have on dry land about the theory of it. That may seem obvious, but it is the initial experiences which prove most disheartening. How many people have felt like giving up after their first lesson in learning any skill? You must be convinced that praying is worth doing or you will be sorely tempted to give up. Do you really believe it is essential that you pray? That you have power from God? That you can be involved in praying down God's plan and will upon the earth? If you allow yourself to think, 'It doesn't really matter,' or, 'I won't be missed, someone else will do it,' then Satan is half-way to victory over you. Be prepared for all sorts of distractions and problems you haven't met before. If you mean business with God in prayer, Satan will have to devote more effort against you. Maybe you have never caused him much concern before!

All the following chapters can be said to contain additional information on how to pray. However, there are certain basic matters that can be covered immediately.

Position

Should I sit or should I kneel? In the time of Jesus it was the custom to stand to pray! 'The Pharisee stood up and prayed (Lk 18:11). A godly bishop used to walk his garden each day as he prayed.

There is no 'should' or 'ought'. For those fortunate enough to have been taught from a child to kneel by their bed there may be such a deep association between kneeling and prayer that they will not find the true contentment and ease of mind unless they kneel. Others may prefer to sit at a table resting their arms on it. Many prefer to use a firm, straight-backed chair and sit upright with their hands resting on their knees—possibly with their palms open and upwards, ready symbolically to receive all that God has for them. The important thing is to be in such a position that we are sufficiently comfortable to forget our bodies but not so comfortable that we fall asleep. Many church pews are so uncomfortable that some people have come to believe that unless they ache somewhere they cannot be truly praying!

For myself, I kneel for part of my prayer time and sit for the rest. When I stopped to analyse where the change of position came, I realized that I kneel for my opening time of worship as I concentrate upon my relationship with God; I sit when I begin to intercede for others.

It seems that in Christ's time it was usual to pray with the eyes open. We read of our Lord himself, 'Then Jesus looked up and said, "Father..."' (Jn 11:41). Many today find that a distraction, but it need not be so. It may help to look at an object or a picture to focus our minds and motivate our thoughts.

Language

Many find it helpful to use the prayers of others handed down the centuries; or more modern books of prayers by such people as Michel Quoist. Even if you do not use them regularly, it can help to stimulate the imagination as we discover ideas which may never have occurred to us otherwise.

To others such a form of praying would be utterly false. For them, all prayer *must* be spontaneous and in their own words. However, we must be careful that we do not despise what others find helpful and effective for them, nor force our opinion on them. We are all different; that is the beauty of God's plan in creation. Maybe you will find it unbearably restrictive to use the words of another in your prayer. But perhaps someone else will find in them a genuine release, expressing exactly what he wants to say. Let us be slow to judge. After all, they are praying to God, not us; let him decide. God is too great and rich for us to confine him to any one individual's limited ways and understanding.

However, whether or not we use the prayers of other people, we should be able to pray in our own words: and let us be sure they are *our* words, not those borrowed from some great preacher of the last century because they sound particularly 'holy'. Surely it does not delight God if we say to our friend, 'I hope you have a good trip,' but then pray, 'Grant them, I beseech thee, gracious Lord, of thy goodness, journeying mercies.'

Let us be real and natural with our heavenly Father, who knows us through and through. Scripture tells us:

> The Lord would speak to Moses face to face, as a man speaks with his friend (Ex 33:11).

Many years ago I read in a newspaper of a little girl who wanted to stay up late to see a particular programme on television. Apparently she had prayed about it because when she came to ask permission of her mother and was told that she could, she burst out: 'Good old God; you never let me down.' The reality of that child's relationship with her heavenly Father, simple as it might be, is surely a lesson to us. I am not suggesting we adopt an attitude of being 'pally' with God. Personally I dislike anyone speaking of him as 'the Boss'. But similarly I do not need to adopt a special tone of voice or turn of phrase to speak with him. I am still 'me' when I pray. Shouldn't we, who have been assured that we are his children, be able to use our natural everyday language and speak with God face to face as a child speaks to his or her earthly father?

There is also the question of whether we should pray silently or by speaking. Again, there are no 'rules' about it. Certainly we do not need to speak out the words for God's benefit. However, it may be very much to our own benefit to do so. It will help concentrate the mind and make our prayers specific.

Perhaps this is the place to mention something akin to the reality of the language we use. That is the reality of the content of our prayer: what we actually pray about. There may be times when we are angry and hurt. If it is because of the action of other people, of course we can and we must bring that to our Father in prayer. Again, we must remember we are little children running to our 'Abba' Father, because we are hurt and need comforting. Far better to go to him than to tell other human beings how unkind so-and-so has been to us.

But what if we are angry at God himself? Suppose we feel that *he* has let us down? I have no hesitation in saying, 'Then tell him how you feel.' There may be those who are horrified at this suggestion. God is the Almighty, holy Creator. Who is man to dare to complain against him? But the first principle in our relationship with God is truth. If we feel angry at God then let us admit it. Although it is wrong to feel like that, it is doubly wrong if we then pretend we don't feel that way. God can take it. If he can take the sin of the whole world on the cross, he can take your anger. You see, while you come and have it out with him, telling him he has failed you and hurt you, you are still very much in relationship with him. You believe he is there to be argued with. God can deal with you while you are taking him seriously like that. What isn't so easy to deal with is the person who feels so let down that he gives up on God altogether. Jeremiah certainly complained to God about the way he had treated him; have a look at Jeremiah 20:7–12, 14–18.

I am no Jeremiah, but perhaps I may share a personal experience. I never wanted to be ordained and when I knew God was calling me to this, I fought against it as long as I could. Finally I surrendered but told him that he would have to change my attitude. Once I had agreed to obey he did change my attitude overnight and I think I have never desired anything so much in all my life. However, when I met with a particular bishop to discuss the matter, he was utterly disheartening. I don't blame him: my health record looked appalling. Active TB in both lungs seven years previously with twelve months off work. A further breakdown in one lung five years later. I had only been back at work eighteen months. It was only because I insisted that I knew God had called me that the bishop agreed to submit my name. However, he as good as told me I had no hope at all of getting through. I am sure he did it to spare me later disappointment, but I returned home shattered and feeling I would be an invalid all my life. That night I knelt down and really let God have it. I reminded him that I had never wanted to be ordained; that it was his idea and I had gone through all that battle for nothing. What was more, I was obviously going to be marked as a sick man all my life. It was a mixture of disappointment, frustration and anger and I poured it all out in bitter complaint at the way he had treated me.

When I came to an end he spoke. It was another of those very, very rare occasions when I heard his voice in my mind. The tone of voice was a sharp rebuke: 'Look, you have given your life to me. If I say you will be well, you will be well. If I say you will be ill, you will be ill. It has nothing to do with doctors or bishops.' It was exactly what I needed. Not so much the telling-off, but the utter certainty and reliability of God's hand on my life. I was taking God seriously and pouring out my heart. I had brought my complaint to the right quarter and he could deal with it and with me.

Incidentally, I got through my medical with no problem. I was held up for two years before I could begin my training because of lack of finance. Eventually I was accepted on the newly formed Southwark Ordination Course. This meant I had to hold down my job in insurance while I studied at evening lectures, weekends and two of my three weeks' annual holiday. Not the best method for an invalid!

So, as I say, be real with God in your prayers. It may very well be that later you will have to apologize for your attitude and confess that it was sin. But understand that it is the *attitude* that is wrong, not the admitting it in your prayer. To try to hide or ignore it is hypocrisy. I am not encouraging you to indulge in tantrums but to come to God not only in spirit but in truth (Jn 4:24).

To whom do we pray?

The basic teaching of Scripture is that we pray

in	the Spirit
through	the Son
to	the Father

Certainly Jesus taught his disciples to address their prayers to the Father, saying: 'When you pray, say: "Father"' (Lk 11:2). This is in line with his other teaching that the Spirit's work is not to speak on his own authority, but to glorify Jesus (Jn 16:13–14) and the work of Jesus is to bring us to the Father.

There are two statements in Scripture on this matter which, at first sight, may appear to conflict with each other. In the first, John 16:26–27, Jesus tells his disciples that he will not need to pray to the Father for them. In the second, Hebrews 7:25, we are told that Jesus does continually intercede for those who come to God through him. As always, when Scripture seems to contradict itself, the solution lies in seeking to understand more deeply what it actually says. So let us examine the texts more carefully.

> In that day you will ask in my name. I am not saying that I will ask the Father on your behalf. No, the Father himself loves you because you have loved me and have believed... (Jn 16:26–27).

What Christ is saying there is that we are no longer sinners cut off from the Father and needing Jesus to plead on our behalf because we do not have access to him ourselves. That would be like a naughty child who has broken a window saying to someone else, 'You go and tell him for me; I'm scared.' As we have seen in the previous chapter, Christ's redeeming work is complete and so utterly effective that we can now come in our own right into the Father's presence. Of course, that right is not by our own merit but won for us by Jesus Christ. That is why we have access to the Father only through Jesus and why our prayers are only through him or in his name. But we can speak with the Father directly.

> Therefore he [Jesus] is able to save completely those who come to God through him, because he always lives to intercede for them (Heb 7:25).

Just because Jesus has won the right for us to have direct personal access to his Father, that does not mean he has ceased to pray for us. After all, I used to pray for my children when they were young. I certainly have not ceased to pray for them now that they are old enough to pray for themselves. So it is with Christ. Indeed he, as our brother, adds his longing and intercession to our own before the Father's throne.

It is important that we don't become too self-conscious about all this. While it would seem both sensible and right

114

to follow scriptural teaching to pray in the Spirit, through the Son, to the Father, don't let us be hampered by some guilt complex if we do not always get the procedure exactly right. God is too big for that.

Praying to and for the dead

Some Christians come from a tradition where they have been taught to pray to departed saints and loved ones or to the Virgin Mary. I have discovered that sometimes other Christians are so disturbed by this that they spend more time trying to convince these people they are wrong than in concentrating on their own prayers. Do not allow their custom to upset *your* relationship with God just because you do not agree with them.

However, Scripture does not give us any encouragement to pray to or through anyone but our Lord; quite the opposite, in fact:

> For there is...one mediator between God and men, the man Christ Jesus (1 Tim 2:5).

My personal reluctance to pray to or through anyone else is more practical than doctrinal. If we have direct access to the Father through Jesus, why do we need to pray to any other being? That seems a very poor second best.

With regard to praying for the dead, personally I do not do this. If they die believers, then they are with Christ in far greater light, joy and blessing than I can imagine. It seems wrong to me to ask that light perpetual may shine upon them—that sounds as though I doubt that it does. If they die as unbelievers I do not believe my prayers can affect anything.

Man is destined to die once, and after that to face judgement (Heb 9:27).

I must leave them to the just and almighty God who is also love. I have no idea what I am praying for if I pray for the dead.

However, I have met some Christians, especially from the evangelical tradition, who are so scared that they might find themselves praying *for* the dead that they cut the departed out of their prayers altogether. What a loss that is. We, above all, can be certain of eternal life. Let us remember the communion of saints; the fact that in Christ we are united with our loved ones who have died in the Lord. Let us praise God that they are not dead, but alive in him. Let us keep their memory alive in joy and let us share that joy with the Lord.

9

Worship, Praise and Thanksgiving

Worship

Some years ago I heard a discussion on the radio about religion. One of the panel was a famous actor. He said he did not believe in God and was revolted by the idea of a supreme being who was so self-centred that he demanded that his subjects should bow down and constantly tell him how wonderful he was.

That, of course, is a total misrepresentation of what we mean by worship. When we worship God we are proclaiming to him, to ourselves, to the world and to the heavenly powers, who we believe him to be. The basis of worship is the conviction 'Our God reigns'. The world is society organized, (or disorganized) apart from God. No wonder so much in the world is wrong and does not function as it should. To worship is part of what is involved in standing in the gap. It is proclaiming, in effect, there *is* a God and he is on the throne. When we worship God we are saying, 'Whatever anyone else believes or desires, we know that you are the King. We want you to rule over us.' Worship has to do with worthship; giving God his rightful place. We declare that God has a plan for this world and that he has authority to bring that plan into being. He is the almighty Creator. The world does not recognize that, but we do, and the moment we do, our immediate response must be to bow down and worship.

If we truly appreciate just who God is, this will affect every aspect of our lives. We will recognize that our possessions are not truly ours at all. We will use them, including our money, to bring glory to God. That is worship. We will appreciate in a new way, just how selfish or arrogant we have been and we will beg God to forgive us. That is worship. We will long that others see the same truth about God that we have seen and we will seek to bring them to acknowledge his rule also. That is worship. Our hearts will overflow with gratitude that he, who is so great and holy, loves us so much and we will express our thanks both in words (thanksgiving) and in what we do (service). That is worship.

Paul explains:

> I urge you... in view of God's mercy, to offer your bodies as living sacrifices, holy and pleasing to God—which is your spiritual worship (Rom 12:1).

As someone remarked, 'The problem with being a *living* sacrifice is that we keep getting up off the altar and walking away.'

So worship is much more than praying but it includes prayer. It does not necessarily require words. One of the Hebrew words translated 'worship' means 'bowing down' and in its most sublime form our initial response renders us speechless. Time and again in Scripture when someone sees the glory of God, he falls flat on his face. The effect is overwhelming.

Occasionally at prayer, I have been aware of the presence of God in a particularly real way. It seems that such a manifestation has nothing to do with how I feel or the manner or fervour of my prayers; it is a sovereign act of grace. When that has happened I have felt constrained to lie down flat on my face. The last thing I have wanted to do is formulate any words or even think of anything except to enjoy God and the state in which I find myself. Those occasions are all too rare. But that is the heart of worship. He is the Creator and I am his creation and, speechless, I adore.

I spoke of enjoying God. That is another description of worship. Most people desire to share their happiness with others. Indeed sharing is part of the happiness. The person who buys a new car will take it round to a friend and invite him to come for a drive. Not just to show off but so that someone else enjoys it with him. At a birthday or anniversary, we may take family or friends to the theatre or out for a meal. It just isn't the same if we do these things alone. Similarly, God delights in his creation.

The first chapter of Genesis tells us he looked at everything he had made and found it good. He wants us to enjoy it with him. Sometimes, when I find an unusual and beautiful flower I will remark, 'Oh isn't that lovely,' and I imagine God saying, 'I thought you would like that.' God wants us to enjoy all he has made, but the very greatest thing he has to share is himself. So, by instructing us to worship him, God is not feeding his own conceit but inviting us to enjoy him. Two people in love enjoy being in each other's company. That is why the first commandment is that we are to love God with all that we have and all that we are. It is not so much a legal demand as an invitation to share ourselves with our Creator who longs to share himself with us.

Praise

Praise, of course, is closely linked to worship because it is a verbal expression of our adoration. The difference between praise and thanksgiving that I would like to draw is that the first is our response to who God is, whereas the latter is our response to what he has done.

In human relationships we need to express our feelings. We may not always find it easy to do so, but the need is there. When someone falls in love, he needs to say so. It isn't just that the beloved likes to hear it, *he* needs to express it. We saw in chapter 5 how rapidly we run out of suitable words to express our deepest feelings. Nevertheless, we do need words. We need to *say*, 'I love you.' If we really fall in love with God we will need to express that in words. That is praise.

There is a strange thing about praise—it is infectious. Very often we may not feel like worshipping God. Of course we ought to, but facts do not always match theories or ideals. However the decision, the cold act of will to praise God, can spark off a glorious time of worship. It is like the starter motor in a car which causes the engine to turn over and fire. By speaking out the truths about God which we accept as facts, whatever our feelings, our hearts are warmed and our spirits begin to function.

Paul gives the following advice:

> Let the word of Christ dwell in you richly as you teach and admonish one another with all wisdom, and as you sing psalms, hymns and spiritual songs with gratitude in your hearts to God (Col 3:16).

From its context that verse obviously refers to worship when the local Christians come together. However, the principle holds good for us as individuals also. Why should the great hymns and choruses be confined to the times when we meet with other Christians? Use a hymn book or a chorus book and sing out. Some Christians use a tape-recorder with a pre-recorded cassette and sing along with it. Beware, however, that it does not simply become a good 'sing-along'. Make sure the word of Christ really does dwell in you richly and that you are meditating on what you are singing. Personally, I prefer not to use a cassette. I am free to sing at the speed I desire, and I can alter the rhythm to linger over a particular word or phrase, to dwell on the meaning.

Over recent years the Lord has given his people many new hymns and choruses. They may not all have the same literary quality as some of the great hymns of the past. Nevertheless, they are a wonderful means of expressing the praise in our hearts. Here is just one example:

> Jesus, we enthrone you,
> We proclaim you our King.
> Standing here in the midst of us
> We raise you up with our praise.
> And as we worship, build a throne,
> And as we worship, build a throne,
> And as we worship, build a throne,
> Come Lord Jesus and take your place.

Paul Kyle. Copyright © Thankyou Music 1977.

If I sing that when I am alone, it does not worry me that it is all in the plural. I am aware that there are many others in heaven and on earth who acknowledge his rule, and I stand with them. Maybe some learned theologians would wish to argue that *we* do not enthrone Jesus, it was his Father who did that. But that is to miss the point. That chorus perfectly illustrates what I was explaining earlier about the nature of worship. It is God's people set in the midst of a world which has gone far from him, proclaiming that our God reigns. God *has* a voice on earth speaking out the truth—ours, yours and mine.

Some of my friends tell me that they make up their own

choruses and tunes to praise the Lord. This is wonderful. What I am saying in all of this is be imaginative, experiment in your prayer times, don't get in a rut.

Another stimulus to praise is the word of Scripture itself. There are many psalms, particularly among numbers 92–108, which are very helpful. And the last five psalms, 146–150, all begin with the words 'Praise the Lord'.

It is a good thing to start our prayer time with praise: even before we confess our sins, unless there is a particular burden to be dealt with immediately. Praise puts God first, where he should be.

Thanksgiving

I remember when, as a child, my mother used to collect me from parties and would always ask, 'Have you said thank you?' I suspect we don't always remember to say thank you to God for what he does for us, particularly for answered prayer. It is not simply a matter of being polite or even grateful, important as that is. Thanksgiving actually aids our praying.

On one occasion I visited one of the house groups we have in our fellowship. It was one which had developed a very real prayer ministry. I was intrigued when one of the members produced a small exercise book and read out all the matters for which they had prayed when they had last met two weeks previously. Others chipped in with their comments, giving information about the outcome of the various items as he went through them. Every prayer had been answered! I am not saying that happened every week in such a dramatic and rapid way, but when the leader called us to prayer for the matters before us that week, there was a sense of expectancy and authority in our prayers. We had just been reminded how effective prayer can be.

Thanksgiving gives God the glory due to him and helps us recall and recognize his blessings. Unfortunately, we don't always see in the events of every day just how our prayers have been answered. There is a story of a workman on a roof who slipped and found himself sliding down the tiles. He cried out to God to help him. Immediately his progress was halted and he said, 'Oh don't bother, God, my braces have caught on a nail.'

Thanksgiving will remind us of our dependency on God. Christ taught us to pray daily for that day's bread. Do we remember to say thank you? To say 'grace' at meals is a very beautiful custom. Once again it is proclaiming 'Our God reigns' every time we eat. If we have invited others to share a meal with us, this simple act of worship can be a very real witness as to what God means to us. Some Christians get into difficulties about saying grace when they are in company. Of course, you must decide for yourself what is right for you before the Lord. We have a simple guideline in our family. If we have guests in our home, or if I have invited others out to a meal and I am host, I say grace. If I am a guest and it is not the custom of my hosts to say grace, then I say it silently. If there is an opportunity, I bow my head as I do so, but if I think even that would make others feel awkward, I do not.

While we are on the subject, I believe that the host (or the hostess if there is no host) is always the one who should lead grace. Being a clergyman, if I am invited out to a meal, I am often asked to 'say grace'. Unless I know my hosts very well I do as I am told. However, I am sure that even if your guest is a bishop it is the host who should bless God for the food he has provided. Mind you, it need not be extended. Bishops have no particular liking for luke-warm soup.

Praise—for everything?

Over recent years some teachers have encouraged Christians to give praise and thanks to God for everything—no matter what difficulties they are facing. I am sure that there is great benefit in this, but we must be careful that we understand the principle involved. It isn't that we are to thank God *for* some particular tragedy, but certainly we can praise him *in* it. If someone comes to tell me he has just crashed his car, I do not feel that my immediate response should be 'Praise the Lord'—especially if he has crashed it into mine. If we are not careful, by following such teaching we may find ourselves praising God for the tragic breakdown of a marriage.

We *can* praise God for the fact that he is the one who has overcome the world and, in Christ, we also will overcome. Once again we are back to the basis of worship—our God reigns. When we are 'going through it', we need to ask ourselves:

Do I believe God reigns?	—if so, nothing can happen to me except he permit it.
If he permits it	—it must be for a purpose.
If it is his purpose	—will I one day praise him for this experience?
If I will praise him one day	—why not praise him now, even before I understand the reason? That is faith.

The psalmist wrote: 'It was good for me to be afflicted' (Ps 119:71). He is looking back to a past event, but the rest of that verse shows that he has come to see that his experience of trouble has been of benefit in his growth as a man of God. So we do not thank God *for* the trouble, in itself—it might in fact be the work of Satan. But we praise God because we believe he can use it.

It is good to worship, to proclaim God reigns, when we see everything is going well. It is even better to proclaim it in the dark, when we cannot see anything at all.

IO

Meditation and Contemplation

We Christians are God's agents on earth. Just as Christ earthed God's will during his ministry, so we are to earth his will today. However, if we are to do that effectively, obviously we must understand what his will is. How can we do that? Some Christians would reply, 'By the Holy Spirit. He guides us into all truth.' Of course, they are right: Scripture itself confirms that (Jn 16:13). But I am concerned that this is sometimes too glib. The guidance of the Holy Spirit is used as a short cut, a spiritual hot-line to God. It seems to me that some of the words of knowledge, wisdom or prophecy I have heard have been the expression of subconscious desires or fears of the individual, rather than the working of the Holy Spirit. I am thrilled that the gifts of the Spirit are once again being revealed and used in the church. However, they need to be used as Scripture lays down. The words spoken by prophets should be weighed and tested by other Christians (1 Cor 14:29). This brings us to another question. How are they to judge whether the words are from God or from a person's subconscious? The answer is that they are to test them by what they know of God (and of the person speaking the prophecy).

Let me illustrate that from everyday family life. Suppose

a father discovers his child about to eat a bar of chocolate half an hour before dinner. He will almost certainly tell him to put it away until after the meal. The child looks up, wide-eyed and says, 'Mummy said I could have it now.' Daddy is not taken in. That does not sound like Mummy. He knows how Mummy thinks because he knows *her*. He has spent time with her.

The gifts of the Holy Spirit are precious and to be encouraged, but they are not a substitute for getting to know God himself. Jeremiah had exactly this problem with the prophets of his day.

> They speak visions from their own minds, not from the mouth of the Lord (Jer 23:16).

Then he gives this explanation:

> Which of them has stood in the council of the Lord to see or to hear his word? (Jer 23:18).

If we want to know God's will we must first get to know God himself. We can do that by meditation and contemplation.

Meditation

This is not the same as general Bible study. It is a special method of thinking about a specific, brief section of God's word and allowing it to dwell in us richly (Col 3:16). It is to take a sentence or even one word and to squeeze every nuance of meaning from it. It is getting the word into our inmost being—and getting us into the word. The psalmist knew what he was about when he said:

> The entrance of your words gives light (Ps 119:130).

The Bible is unlike any other book. It contains not only the words of God but God himself. That statement needs explanation. Words can be a sacrament. To say 'I love you' does not only convey my feeling, it conveys something of *me*. By speaking those words I am sharing my thoughts, my feelings, myself. The nearest I can get to explaining how I regard Scripture is to liken it to those dehydrated dinner packets. When the food is prepared in the factory it has all the moisture taken from it and the dry powder is packed in foil. When I put these dry ingredients into a saucepan and mix them with water, the whole dinner is reconstituted as it warms through. The Bible, I believe, is the very word of God. On the printed page it can seem very dry and uninteresting. But as the Holy Spirit is allowed to work upon it in our minds, so it becomes the living word of God to us.

Meditation cannot be rushed. Suppose you were meditating upon the words 'God so loved the world'. You would first consider the word 'God'. What thoughts would come? Perhaps you would consider him first as Creator. Your mind might run over the stars, the universe, the sea, the soil, the forests, the mountains, the smallest insect. Then you might think of his holiness, his justice, his wisdom and many other aspects of his character. After a while you move on to the little word 'so'. You will need to link it to the word 'loved' but it will lead you to consider the expanse of God's yearning. Then to the word 'loved'. Your thoughts might remind you of a child of your own, and times when you became exasperated with him or her. But God so *loved*. Then you meditate upon 'the world'. How is it organized? What has it done to God's creation? What have I done to it? What have we done to God? Where do we put him? Yet what is his attitude to us?—he so loved! What is *my* attitude to the world?

In this way we change from spectators watching God

128

act out his will, and we become his people actively involved in what he is doing on earth. Meditation draws us to God's mind so that we begin to see things as he sees them, think as he thinks.

Finding texts for meditation

How can we decide what to meditate on? One way is simply to be still before God and ask him to lead us to a book in the Bible. When we feel that perhaps he is saying such and such we can then begin to read slowly until a particular text jumps out at us, or takes our attention. An alternative is to record a chapter or a short book onto a cassette. At our time of meditation, we can ask God to lead us to a text and then listen to the tape until a phrase or word gets hold of us in a particular way.

Personally I find the book *Daily Light* very useful. It is a well-known publication with selected Scripture texts on a given theme for each morning and evening. Or again, I remember when I felt there was a particular weakness in my character, I spent several weeks meditating on the fruit of the Spirit in Galatians 5:22. I took a word at a time, considering what it really meant and picturing myself in various situations and how I would (or should) react. I imagined the Spirit within me, working upon my mind and heart.

Another suggestion is to look up the various 'names' of God in Scripture and think of the implications they reveal of his character.

Meditation gets the word into our inner being where it can explode and impregnate every part. To adapt a well-known advertisement: the word of God refreshes the parts that other words cannot reach.

Perhaps I should add a word of warning. Meditation is important, but it should not replace other methods of using Scripture. I could not live on a diet of *Daily Light*. I need to read larger chunks of the Bible as well, to follow the overall thrust of an argument or train of thought.

Contemplation

If meditation is to seek to learn more of God through letting his word dwell in us richly, contemplation is to seek to know God as he is in himself, without using Scripture as the springboard for our thoughts. This is not to place Scripture on a lower or higher plane than contemplation; they are just different.

The basis of contemplation for me is summed up in the words, 'Be still, and know that I am God' (Ps 46:10). The wonderful thing about a good father is that he will know each of his children individually. He will act and respond to them, and they to him, in a way which is unique for each individual child. That is true also of our relationship with our heavenly Father. We must develop our relationship with him in the way that is just right for us. We explored this to some extent in considering our heritage and the use of our imagination. Great and detailed books have been written by men and women well experienced in contemplation and the more mystical aspects of prayer. This is not the place to attempt to enter this area in detail and I am certainly not proficient to do it. However, it may be helpful to set out a few basic principles related to contemplation.

Consider your breathing. In both the Old and New Testaments there is a common word for both 'spirit' and 'wind'. God's 'breath and 'spirit' are regarded as interchangeable. After his resurrection Jesus *breathed* on his disciples and said, 'Receive the Holy Spirit' (Jn 20:22). You may find it helpful to begin a time of prayer, and especially contemplation, by consciously breathing slowly and deeply, and imagining the Spirit of God filling you.

Here perhaps I should add a warning about certain techniques associated with yoga and transcendental meditation. Although these may at first appear harmless or even beneficial, their roots are in oriental, non-Christian religions. In contemplation we are not 'emptying' our minds, for if we do that who knows what may enter them? We are 'surrendering' our minds to God; filling them with thoughts about him; waiting, listening for him. We need first to ask him to take our minds and direct them and reveal himself to us.

Some people find it helps them to begin a time of contemplation by having an object before them; a flower, a painting, a cross. The psalmist used the natural world around him:

> When I consider your heavens, the work of your fingers, the moon and the stars, which you have set in place, what is man that you are mindful of him? (Ps 8:3).

or

> I lift up my eyes to the hills... (Ps 121:1).

Wandering thoughts

We all know this one; it is not something which only you experience. So do not lose heart. There are a number of things to be said.

Are you sure they are wandering?

You may want to reply, 'Of course I am sure. As soon as I try to be still and think of God, all sorts of thoughts crowd into my mind and I get distracted.' Next time that happens, stop and check exactly what you have been 'distracted' by. It may be that just as you were settling down to consider the majesty of God, you found yourself thinking about some relative who has been impossible recently. You are convinced she had more than her fair share of someone's will, or you know she thinks you did and.... At that point you recall you are trying to contemplate and you drag your mind back, saying 'Sorry, Father, I got distracted.' But perhaps you did not. Maybe this is the first time for months that God has managed to set one of *his* thoughts in your busy mind. Before you try to offer God pious and holy acts of devotion, he is asking you to sort out your resentment and bitterness against your relative. If there has been a breakdown in your relationship, it may be that God is seeking to encourage you to do all you can to restore it.

> If you are offering your gift at the altar and there remember that your brother has something against you, leave the gift there in front of the altar. First go and be reconciled to your brother; then come and offer your gift (Mt 5:23–24).

Make a written note

Sometimes when we stop being busy and turn to prayer our subconscious mind throws up matters which do need to be dealt with, *but not then*. 'Put the dustbin out', 'telephone the dentist', 'return the library book'. Don't just hope you will remember it later, jot it down on a slip of paper. Then you will be truly free to return to your prayer.

Turn the distraction into prayer

If it is a bird singing—thank God for creation. If it is a neighbour's radio—pray for the media and picture the neighbour. What are his needs, his hopes, his potential?

Evil thoughts

Above all, do not despair. Do not try to deal with them by yourself. You probably won't find it at all helpful to try to push them out of your mind. Share them with Jesus. Admit to him what is happening and face the thoughts together in a positive way. 'Lord, I'm planning revenge against...You didn't think like that as they drove in the nails.' Picture the person and begin to think of him as you know Christ thinks of him. Deal with lustful thoughts in the same way. Share these with Christ, seeking his help. Jesus knows what it is like to be tempted; he 'has been tempted in *every* way, just as we are—yet was without sin' (Heb 4:15). No one has seriously suggested Jesus was undersexed. He learned how to direct his sexuality as God intended, and he can do that for you. Remember, it isn't wrong to be tempted with evil thoughts, but it is wrong to give them board and lodging.

Listening to God

We have seen how, in the beginning, man was able to communicate with God. Not only could he speak to God, he could hear or comprehend what God wanted to say to him. As a result of the fall, man lost his ability to hear God. Nevertheless, one or two selected people in each age were able to receive his voice, for God did not leave himself without witness. It was the task of those prophets to interpret God's will to the whole people. Since the coming of Christ, however, this ability to hear God has been restored. In his description of himself as the Good Shepherd, Jesus speaks four times of the fact that his sheep, those who follow him, will hear and recognize his voice (Jn 10:3–4, 16, 27).

Jesus developed this teaching in greater detail on the

last night of his earthly ministry. Judas had already left to
betray him and Jesus knew that he had so much more to
teach his true disciples, but they just could not take any
more at that time (Jn 16:12). However, the fact that he
was about to be taken from them and killed, rise again and
return to his Father in heaven, did not mean that they
would no longer receive his guidance. Far from it; he
explained:

> When he, the Spirit of truth, comes, he will guide you into all
> truth...He will bring glory to me by taking from what is mine
> and making it known to you (Jn 16:13–14).

So Jesus was clearly teaching that his followers would
know what he desired because it would be revealed to
them by the Holy Spirit. The full truth is even more
wonderful than that. We are actually to be allowed into
the counsels of God. It is important that we understand
what Jesus meant if we are to fulfil our ministry of 'standing
in the gap'. The teaching comes in the time which he had
with the disciples in the upper room after Judas had left
and before they went to the Garden of Gethsemane. You
will find it in John 15:14–17. Jesus explains that those who
really love him will obey him. If they do what he
commands, then they are his friends. He no longer regards
them as servants, but friends. The difference between the
two is that a servant may well not understand the reason
for an order he has been given, he is simply to carry it out.
But with a friend, says Jesus, you share the reason or
purpose which lies behind the command.

Sometimes, on my day off, my wife and I will go to
Dover, to the cliffs above the docks and watch the cross-
channel ferries come in and out. They back into their
berths at quite a speed. At the last minute, so it seems, the
captain orders the engines to be changed from 'astern' to

'ahead', just for a few seconds, and the great ship slides gently to a halt with a few feet to spare. The engineer below cannot see anything of what is happening. That does not matter. His task is to obey immediately and implicitly the command of his superior officer on the bridge. He fulfils the role of the servant.

As soldiers in Christ's S.A.S. it is our task to obey his commands without question. However, he no longer regards us as servants only. To adapt the metaphor, he has invited us to stand on the bridge with him. We are still to serve and obey his commands, but we are to understand something, at least, of the purpose which lies behind them. He tells his disciples:

> I have called you friends, for everything that I learned from my Father I have made known to you (Jn 5:15).

Then, in case we have not grasped the reason for this great privilege of sharing in the counsels of God, Jesus explains it is for the very purpose of enabling us to 'stand in the gap'. He says that we did not choose him but he chose us to bear fruit, fruit that will last.

> Then the Father will give you whatever you ask in my name (Jn 15:16).

Are you now beginning to believe that you are one of God's chosen ones, and the purpose for which he has chosen you is to ask and receive from the Father? In a sentence: you have been chosen to stand in the gap!

It is not easy to explain just how God speaks to us. It is like trying to answer the question, 'How do I know if I'm in love?' All you can say is 'You will know!' Different people experience God in different ways. Do understand, however, that if God desires to put a thought into your mind then, of course, he does have only your mind to put it into. That is to say, *you* will think of something. Just because it is you thinking it, do not assume that it cannot be from God. Once the thought is in your mind it becomes your thought. The important factor is where did that thought spring from? Was it put there by someone else—something you heard someone say? Did it spring from your own subconscious mind? Or did it come from God's Holy Spirit through your spirit? In each case it is you who end up thinking it. With experience you will learn to distinguish which thoughts come from yourself and which come from God. As Jesus promised, his sheep do learn to recognize his voice.

Nevertheless, there are certain guidelines which may be helpful as you seek to distinguish his voice and know his will.

God's word

God will not direct you in a way contrary to his will as it is already revealed in Scripture. I remember a couple sitting in my home assuring me that God had brought them together. Their relationship was so wonderful. The man had left his wife and children to enter into this 'wonderful' relationship. God has a word for that: adultery. He also says, 'Thou shalt not.'

God's character

Is the 'guidance' we think we have received in accordance with what we know of God? This is where we need to build up our understanding of God and his ways through meditation on his word.

Advice from mature Christians

If they *are* mature they will not seek to decide for you—unless your proposed actions are downright sinful. Talking with them may help clarify the issue. Of course, even mature Christians are fallible; there may be occasions when they get it wrong. I am convinced that if Moses had waited for a majority vote in his church council, the Israelites would never have crossed the Red Sea! However, do not lightly dismiss the advice of others who are walking in God's ways.

Make sure your hands are off the scales

That is to say, while you are weighing up possible courses of action, beware that your own preference is not dominating the decision. On the other hand, do not go to the opposite extreme of assuming that God will always demand the exact opposite of what you would like. The more Christlike you become, the more his plans will delight you.

Is there peace in your heart?

When you decide on a course of action, even if it is awe-inspiring, do you feel at peace about it? Paul said: 'Let the peace of Christ rule in your hearts' (Col 3:15). In its context that is referring to relationships within the fellowship. However, it is a useful guide. The word 'rule' really means 'act as umpire'. If you are uneasy in your innermost being, that may well be God's indication that something is wrong.

(Sanctified) common sense

If you are already in debt and someone offers you a car at a bargain price, your common sense hardly needs to be sanctified to know you cannot buy it.

Let me stress that these are guidelines, not commandments. God is sovereign and we can all think of great men and women of God who have gone against most of those

137

guidelines because they have been convinced they have heard God call them in some definite way. Fortunately, the call has been so clear and they have learnt to recognize their master's voice so surely, that all has been well. Most of us are not yet in such a position.

One last comment. Occasionally someone will delay too long before he acts because he is waiting for a specific word from God. Such people often quote Isaiah 30:21— 'Whether you turn to the right or to the left, your ears will hear a voice behind you, saying, "This is the way; walk in it."' But in Scripture the way of the Lord is a straight way. To go to the right or left is to go off course. It is *then* that you hear a voice of correction—'This is the way.' There are times when we pray and seem to get no firm guidance. Provided we are truly desiring to go his way, we may just have to trust we are moving in the right direction and he will shut the doors we are not to go through.

11

What to Pray For

If you are not used to intercession you may wonder how to fill your prayer time. As you become practised you will wonder what you can leave out!

Think beforehand what you really do intend to pray for. The idea seems to have got around that somehow it is particularly spiritual to be vague and totally unplanned. It may well be right to ask God to reveal what he desires you to pray about; but that is not the same thing at all. That is a definite and clear cut plan in your mind to wait on God. Once you know the subject, you will then need to think through, with the Holy Spirit, just how to pray for it.

It is essential that you are specific. To be *eff*ective, prayer must be *sel*ective. If you pray, 'God bless Africa,' you must be prepared for your heavenly Father to set about helping you grow up and reply, 'Certainly, in what particular way?' Remember the story of blind Bartimaeus (Mk 10:46 ff). When he heard that Jesus was passing by, he cried out for him to have mercy. Jesus called him, and when he stood before him asked, 'What do you want me to do?' Surely that was obvious, but he waited for the man to specify exactly what he wanted—to have his sight restored. And notice the place of faith in that healing.

There are two obvious reasons why we need to be

specific. First of all it has to do with our key position in the plan of God revealed at the very beginning of Scripture: we are to exercise authority—lordship—on earth. We are to direct the power of God onto a particular person, group or event and 'see' it happen. It is difficult to picture clearly in our minds God 'blessing' Africa! The second reason why we need to be specific is that if we are not clear what we are praying for it will not be easy to recognize the answer when it comes.

Some suggestions

I find it helpful to use a prayer list. The way I prepare mine is to set out a number of headings on a sheet of paper. These are such subjects as relatives, colleagues, church, government, missionaries, media, authorities, and so on. Under each heading I will write the names of the different people involved.

The first two headings cause no difficulty; you will know who should be included in your own list. Under 'church' I enter my bishop and his suffragan, my fellow elders and their wives, our curate and our community worker, and others. Presumably you will include your pastor or minister. Under 'government' you may like to include the Prime Minister and Cabinet but, just as important, you should include your own M.P. and local government councillors. Under 'media' there will be your local radio station, television and newspaper, as well as wider national issues like censorship and pornography. 'Authorities' is a general term under which I include education and health. This embraces particular schools in the area, teachers within the church fellowship with whom we have a special relationship, and also my doctor and dentist.

I then take seven sheets of paper to be filed in a loose-leaf notebook. I write a different day of the week on each and select one or two names or items from each subject-heading to be entered on each sheet. In this way I have a variety of subjects every day to pray for and all the individual matters are covered each week. If you have a great number of topics, you may prefer to divide them into thirty and pray for each on a monthly basis. I use both systems. One particularly helpful aid is the list of our church membership produced annually. We give a copy to every member. It is a simple matter to divide the total by thirty and pray for a group, individually, each day of the month.

I must stress, of course, that it is important that we really do pray for the people involved and not just recite a list of subjects or names. For myself, I picture the person as I pray, recalling what I know of them; their needs, problems and joys. With people I do not know well, M.P.s and officials, I try to remember that they have families and homes and are subject to the same stresses and responsibilities as the rest of us, as well as the particular pressures of their work.

There may be some Christians who just cannot manage with such a prayer list. They find it restrictive, turning prayer into a chore which has to be accomplished. I understand this and maybe they will find some other method which suits them. However, I find I cannot rely on my memory or trust my inclination to pray regularly for matters which I believe require it. If so much of God's plan depends on man praying it down upon earth, surely this is too important for me to depend on what I may remember or may feel like as I come to pray each day.

Having said that, I know only too well that to use the same lists for a long period can become boring. Prayer lists must be kept up to date and changed if we are to pray with enthusiasm.

I know that some Christians carry a note book with them and jot down items for prayer as they arise. They hear of the birth of a child, someone going into hospital, an exam, a new job. They read of something in a magazine or hear of it on radio or television and make a note to pray about it. Maybe they only pray for each item on one occasion before another takes its place.

Most missionary societies and aid organizations publish a bulletin of matters for prayer. There are one or two groups which are not tied to any particular society which publish monthly, bi-monthly or quarterly topics specifically to aid those who engage in regular intercessory prayer. They include the latest information about different nations, or legal, moral and scientific issues which are currently being discussed or introduced. If we are to pray specifically and authoritatively, we need to have facts so that we know what we are about. You may feel it right to ask God to give you a particular nation or field of industry, commerce, or scientific experiment to pray for. This can prove very valuable in promoting lively and effective prayer. You will need to read up all you can on the subject and add to this as news items about it are covered by the media.

I have been praying for China for some time now. I find it is a two-way operation. My prayer burden has increased my interest in news and documentaries about that nation; especially when I see what I believe are answers to prayer in these reports. And the information I gain enlivens and encourages my prayer.

This matter of obtaining information is essential if your prayers are to be meaningful and effective. I am sure that much of my prayer has been less effective than it might have been because I have not thought through the consequences of what I am asking. Let me give you an example.

Mauritania is a country on the West coast of Africa just below Morocco, adjoining Algeria, Mali and Senegal. It has an area of just over 1,000,000 square kilometres and a population of about 1,300,000—compared with Great Britain's area of less than 500,000 square kilometres and a population of over 56,000,000. Most of the land is desert and it is a very poor nation with over half the people living as nomads. There are no known native Christian believers. With those limited facts, I think I would pray for God to raise up missionaries to go into that harvest field. I would pray for Bibles to be sent out and for many to be converted. But now let me give you some more facts. It is an Islamic state with 99% of the population Muslims. Several missions wish to enter but no mission work is allowed. With regard to Bibles, there are no Scriptures translated into the dialects of the country and at present there is little incentive to do anything about this because the great majority of people cannot read anyway. With regard to praying for conversions, apparently there have been two in the past. One was a student in France; nothing has been heard from him since his return to his native Mauritania. The other was a sheikh; he is reported to have been killed for seeking to share the gospel with his people. It may be right to pray for conversions but, if we do, we must appreciate we are probably, in fact, condemning them to death. Now, how do we pray for that situation? 'God bless Africa' is ridiculous in the light of those facts. Each of us must seek the Lord for guidance if we have a burden for that or similar situations. For me the battle lies in the heavenly realms. I have been praying for some time now against the spiritual principalities and powers which control and block the situation in Mauritania.

I believe that if we wait on God, he will reveal how we are to pray for nations like that. However, I also believe he expects us to use our intellect to gather the facts that are available to us if we take the trouble. Most of the details set out above about Mauritania are included in a very useful and comprehensive book, *Operation World* by P.J.Johnstone (Send the Light, the publishing section of Operation Mobilisation). It is subtitled 'A Handbook for World Intercession'. That is exactly what it is, giving detailed information of over 200 countries. Of course in today's world there are many and rapid changes and such a publication is soon out of date. However, the book also includes details of organizations which supply regular information about nations throughout the world.

Praying for leaders

> I urge, then, first of all, that requests, prayers, intercession and thanksgiving be made for everyone—for kings and all those in authority, that we may live peaceful and quiet lives in all godliness and holiness (1 Tim 2:1–2).

It is important to understand the background to Paul's instructions. In Great Britain you may be mocked if you actually go to church, but most people like to be regarded as Christians—at least, they become upset if anyone implies they are *not* Christians. That was not so in Paul's day. Most of the churches to whom he wrote his letters were not large congregations. They were comparatively small groups meeting in different houses. Christians were regarded generally as a rather odd sect who might very well stir up trouble. Probably they were regarded much as punks, skinheads or rockers are today by members of society at large. Yet it was to these numerically small groups that Paul stressed the importance of prayer. Indeed, it was a first priority on his agenda. They were to pray for everyone and kings and leaders in particular. If you think through the implications of what Paul was saying, you will realize that he believed the prayers of a small minority would have a profound effect on history. He obviously considered that Christians could exercise lordship over world events by prayer and he singled out government as a particularly important area.

Occasionally I meet Christians who have a real problem about praying for the world. They point to various texts in Scripture which speak of the destruction of the world; that Christians are to come out of the world into the kingdom of God; that Jesus specifically stated on one occasion that he was not praying for the world (Jn 17:9). These Christians are unable to pray for anything to do with the world except that more people will leave it for the kingdom.

Of course, they are right in the sense that we are not to pray for the existing world order, which is opposed to God, to be upheld or preserved. But there are countless people, events and situations which need God's help and, therefore, the prayers of Christians. No one would deny that Christ taught that man does not live by bread alone. Nevertheless, similarly no one can deny that he fed a multitude with material supplies of bread and fish because he had compassion on them—even though he well knew what was in their hearts, which resulted in all but his disciples leaving him the next day because they found his demands too great.

We live out our present lives in the midst of this world, and that is where we must exercise our Christian ministry. If I come across someone in desperate need and I can do something about it, then it is not for me to enquire first is he a Jew or Samaritan, Communist or Muslim. He is a man made in the image of God; an image which, like mine, has been marred. I have been shown how that image may be restored and I have responded. It may be that I will have the opportunity to share that truth with him later, I do not know. Meanwhile it is sufficient motivation that he is in need. So it is with our prayers.

As I write, there is a jet plane on a tarmac in a foreign country with forty passengers and crew in the hands of fanatical terrorists. They have threatened to kill a hostage every hour unless their demands are met. I have no idea whether there are any Christians involved in the situation, but I believe this is an evil act, contrary to the will of God. The only thing I can do is pray.

Some five or six months ago one of our house groups, waiting on the Lord in prayer, felt led to pray that some of the surplus grain in Europe should be physically shipped out to feed the starving in the third world. More recently in a time of public testimony during our morning service a member of that house group shared his joy at a news item on television the previous evening that farmers in Great Britain were supporting a scheme to 'send a tonne' of this year's harvest to the drought areas of Africa. I am not claiming any credit for ourselves, the glory is all the Lord's, but I do believe he graciously allowed our house group to play a part in his will being fulfilled on earth. Certainly that testimony encouraged the whole fellowship to continue the work of intercession.

To return to the instruction of Paul to pray for everyone, particularly kings and all in authority. He explains that this is so that we may lead peaceful and quiet lives in all godliness and holiness. He goes on to say that this pleases God who longs for all men to be saved and come to know the truth. Surely it is better to have good government than bad. If a government is corrupt it breeds corruption among the people. If it is unjust, then injustice prevails in the land. In the information set out above about Mauritania we saw that part of the problem is that the government will not allow missions to operate in the country. In some nations, Morocco for instance, it is actually illegal for a

Muslim to change his religion. Paul knew what he was talking about when he focused on kings and all in authority.

How much do Christians pray for the government of their own nation? Instead of complaining about the government we have got, let us exercise our authority in prayer to raise up righteous men and women to positions of authority. Let us pray that the unrighteous will be reformed or removed. Of course, I would like all men to be saved, but remember God is able to use unbelievers to fulfil his will. He even speaks of Cyrus, a pagan king, as 'my anointed', because when the Jews were held in exile in Babylonia it was Cyrus whom God raised up in righteousness to permit them to return to their own land (Is 45:1,13).

Many people who are in positions of authority in television, radio, newspapers and publishing, exercise great influence for good or ill. There are men and women of integrity and justice who make no profession of Christian faith, whom God can use. I am not now talking of their salvation but of their influence which promotes the atmosphere in which holiness and godliness may be upheld and demonstrated, and the gospel proclaimed by those who do know God. I have worked on both television and local radio with men and women who do not claim to be Christian, but who have proved to be even more helpful and encouraging than some who do. Oh that Christians would learn to use the power God has given us to rule the world through prayer.

Specific areas of concern

It seems to me that when we pray for any nation, including our own, there are certain issues on which we should concentrate.

147

The church

Again, it is not sufficient to pray 'God bless the church'. We need spiritual leaders who stand in the counsels of God and who have more than natural wisdom. A church whose leaders teach and proclaim the word of God in love but without compromise, and whose members live out the kingdom in their own lives. Of course, as we have seen, some nations do not yet have a church and we must seek God's guidance on how to pray one into being.

The government

Even where it would be totally unrealistic to pray that Christians should be chosen as leaders of the nation, e.g. in the case of totally Communist or Islamic regimes, we can pray for God to raise up righteous men and women so that there may be justice and peace, not only within that nation but in their international relationships.

Education

What we are taught becomes what we believe which, in turn, affects how we live.

The media

Perhaps in some areas this is limited to jungle drums. However, I have in mind the more sophisticated systems in the developed countries. We all know that the same facts can be presented with a different emphasis according to the particular views of the writer, the editor, or producer. Yet most of us form our opinions from what we read, see or hear through the media. In addition there are the attitudes we adopt almost unconsciously from the behaviour of 'stars' and characters in plays or films. Remember the particular pressures on Christians working in this field.

The judicial system

It is vital that truth and justice shall prevail. God has a concern for the poor and the oppressed. There must be redress against those who exploit others.

Health programmes

In many areas of the world there is so much to do to alleviate suffering; yet much *can* be done if only the motivation is there. In parts of Africa and India a comparatively simple operation can restore sight to large numbers of blind people. Instruction in basic hygiene can save many lives. In the West there are frightening ethical issues arising with experiments in the field of genetic engineering.

Family life

In some nations like South Africa the women and children are compelled to live in one area but husbands and fathers live many miles away in order to find suitable employment. In other more affluent nations little importance is attached to building stable family units. God's standards are held in derision.

The economy

This involves widespread issues. The exploitation of poor nations by the rich; unemployment; the availability of water; industry and commerce.

Obviously, that list with its comments is no more than a few suggestions to stimulate your imagination.

As well as your individual prayers, it can be a great encouragement to meet with others and wait on the Lord together so that he can reveal the matters that are on his heart. So often in church prayer meetings everyone comes with his or her bundle of petitions and one follows the other, each totally unconnected to the next and with no time to pray through any matter in depth. I am sure that it is right for a fellowship to pray with and for each other, but I sometimes wonder if at the end God is left wondering why no one thought of asking if *he* had any matters which he desired to put before them for prayer. After all, it seems a little odd to pray, 'Your will be done on earth,' if we never stop to ask what that will is.

12

Into Action

This is the most crucial part of the book. I know myself well enough to realize that if I were reading it instead of writing it I would become diverted at this stage. I would want to talk with other Christians and ask them what they thought. Do they agree with its teaching? I would put it down, telling myself that I must think through the implications in greater depth. I might even feel challenged by certain chapters and decide I really ought to get down to planning a more structured prayer life sometime. My problem would be in actually *doing* anything about it.

I am not so very different from other people and my guess is that you may be diverted in just that way. Let me beg you: don't put this aside without acting on it. It may be that there are some things with which you disagree: that is fine, if it has helped you clarify what you believe and why you believe it. Perhaps the ideas and suggestions which have helped me will hinder you and you will reject them. That doesn't matter. What is important is that you pray; that your relationship with God is real, vital and maintained.

May I make a suggestion? That you decide *now* when you will plan your prayer life. I am not asking when you will actually start doing the praying; simply when you will plan it, because it needs planning. If you attempt to launch into praying without first planning, your interest and enthusiasm will rapidly fail. They may fail anyway, from time to time, which is why you need a structure to discipline and carry you through such periods. So decide now when you will plan your prayer; a time within the next seven days at the most when you can sit down undisturbed and work out what you will do and what you will need. I set out a list of matters you will need to consider. You may find it helpful to write them on a sheet of paper and fill in your decisions.

1. My place of prayer _____

2. I will set aside each day
   for prayer the following
   length of time _____

3. Each day I will begin my
   prayer time at _____

4. I will begin to operate
   this plan on _____

5. I will obtain _____

The first item needs no explanation. With regard to the second, a few things should be said. Be realistic, stretch yourself but not beyond what you can reasonably achieve. I cannot know your situation or problems. However, I would suggest that fifteen minutes is too little but, if you have not had a structured prayer time before, anything over an hour may prove too demanding. Even if you cannot manage an hour to start with I commend that to you as a goal. I have already remarked that I do not believe I have a particular gift or calling as an intercessor, but neither am I an evangelist. I have discovered I am a teacher. However, just because I am not an evangelist that does not mean that I do not seek to share my faith with others and encourage them to find Christ for themselves. Similarly, although I am not an intercessor, that does not mean I do not intercede. We all have a responsibility for intercession. It may be that for some of our relatives, friends or colleagues, we are the only Christian who knows of the situation and we are the only one who can stand in the gap between heaven's supply and their particular need.

I am praying that God will use this book to show some that he has called them to a *ministry* of intercession. Over recent years God has been calling small groups of women to this ministry in 'Lydia' fellowships, where two or three or more gather in his name, wait on the Lord together and intercede under the guidance of the Holy Spirit. It is helpful to meet with others in this way, but it is certainly not the only way of intercession. I hardly need to say that just because we have a set time for prayer, that does not mean we cannot use other occasions also. Many routine jobs do not require all our concentration—ironing, washing-up, painting and decorating; certainly we can be praising, meditating and interceding while we do these things.

Remember, intercession is work, hard work. Personally, when I am on holiday while I keep a regular prayer time, I cut back on my intercession considerably. I find I need a break from that as much as I do from sermon preparation, the telephone and caring for the parish.

The third item on the list relates to the time at which you will begin your prayers each day. Remember you will have to *make* time, you will not *find* it. Review your day; work out when you have to be doing something else—

leaving to catch a bus or meeting the children from school—and work backwards from there.

I have put in the fourth heading for the same reason that I suggested you set a time to do the planning. It is so easy to have good intentions but to miss out on the action. Do not leave it too long or your resolve will weaken as the days go by. However, you will need to get one or two things together, which brings us to the final item.

You may require:

for praise:	music tapes, chorus books, selected psalms.
meditation:	taped Bible readings, *Daily Light*, selected scriptures.
contemplation:	a picture, a flower, a cross (beware, for some these are a distraction).
intercession:	prayer list, books or pamphlets of information, daily newspaper items, note book.

It may be helpful to recall the different areas you may wish to include in your prayer time.

praise
meditation
thanksgiving
contemplation
confession
petition
intercession

That is only a guide and must never become a rigid rule. Use it with imagination and intersperse praise and thanksgiving along the way.

Finally, let me encourage you to stick at it for at least a month once you begin. I do not mean you should then stop, but we are creatures of habit. If you will decide that, come what may, you will keep to your plan for a month, you will find it is much easier to continue it in future. It will become part of your life, and surely that is what prayer should be.

Epilogue

In the first chapter I pointed out that when God created man he instructed him to fill the earth and subdue it. I mentioned that this seemed rather strange. If anything needed to be subdued we might expect God to have done it. It is as though the work of creation was not complete. That cannot have been by mistake because when God reviewed all he had done he found it very good. Therefore there must have been some purpose in God's decision to leave this subjection undone.

What was that purpose? I believe it was for man to cut his teeth, so to speak. It is to do with man exercising lordship, learning to use the authority of God which he has been given. We are being trained here on earth during our lifetime for an eternal destiny. We are the chosen bride of Christ. We know that even now while we are in the body on earth, we have been raised spiritually to sit with Christ in the heavenly realm. The day of the marriage feast of the Lamb will come (Rev 19:7) and we will reign with Christ (Rev 22:3–5). Paul tells us that we are to judge not only the world but angels (1 Cor 6:2–3).

Here and now God needs us and has called us to stand in the gap so that his will may be done on earth as it is in heaven. The world depends on us if its true needs are to be met, even if it does not recognize the fact, because its deepest needs can be met only in Christ. But behind those immediate needs I believe God is working out a more wonderful purpose still. He is preparing us for our future role to reign with Christ. He is teaching us how to wield spiritual power and authority. That was his plan from the very beginning. When man rebelled it looked as though that plan had failed. But God sent his Son in the flesh, the last Adam, to restore what the first Adam, and every other man after him, had lost. We who have made Jesus Lord and Saviour have been chosen as sons of God to live out the kingdom on earth and to rule the world under the authority of God. We are to sway the future by the prayer of faith. Let us take up our high calling and so fulfil the work of Christ to link heaven and earth. God wants his creation back and he has chosen us to see that it is done (Rom 8:18–21).

The Way of an Intercessor

by Audrey Merwood

Throughout the world God is raising up groups of women to explore new depths of intercessory prayer. Audrey Merwood has been privileged to share in this move of God's Spirit, and here she gives practical wisdom and biblical insight into how such a group may operate.

As she shares her experiences from her involvement with the Lydia Fellowship, we see the joys and also the sacrifices involved in treading the way of an intercessor.

'This is a very readable book, instructive yet warm and personal. Audrey identifies with the daily lives of women and shows something of the great prayer potential we all have within us.'
Jeanne Harper

'It is my prayer that all who read this book may know a deeper desire to wait on God to know his heart, and pray his prayers for the church, our own nation and the world.'
Chris Leage
National Co-ordinator Lydia Fellowship

Kingsway Publications

Spiritual Warfare

by Michael Harper

Christians are at war!

Not against flesh and blood, but against
'the spiritual hosts of wickedness in the heavenly
places'.

Spiritual warfare is not glamorous, nor is it for the
'professional few'. Every believer has a part to play
and must be aware of the disciplines involved.

Michael Harper is careful to avoid the snares and
pitfalls of the subject, while yet determined to
expose the enemy in the light of Scripture. He gives
practical advice on how we can all remain vigilant
and be victorious over the enemy, strong in the
authority that the Holy Spirit gives to those who
believe in the Lord Jesus.

k

Kingsway Publications

The Furnace of Renewal
A Vision for the Church

by George Mallone

Renewal — cheap or costly?
— cosmetic or charismatic?
— passing or permanent?

Along with many others, George Mallone longs to see renewal come to the church. But he is convinced God is calling the church of the eighties to submit to a baptism of the Spirit *and* of fire, so that we are equipped and ready to play our part in God's purposes.

'God desires that his name be great among the nations. To accomplish this he has chosen to refine a people to glorify that name. His very reputation is at stake . . . It is through the church that the wisdom of our God is made known to principalities and powers.

The renewal of the church may be within reach for those who are prepared not only to be empowered but also refined by the Spirit.'

Kingsway Publications